T0360854

Why REDD will Fail

Reducing Emissions from Deforestation and Forest Degradation (REDD) attempts to address climate change from one angle – by paying developing countries to slow or stop deforestation and forest degradation. Trumpeted as a way to both mitigate climate change and assist countries with development, REDD was presented as a win–win solution. However, there have been few attempts to understand and analyze the overall framework.

Why REDD will Fail argues that the important goals will not be met under the existing REDD regime unless the actual drivers of deforestation and forest degradation are diminished. The book delves into the problematic details of the regime, ranging from national capacity to monitor the results to the funding mechanism, the definition of a forest, leakage, and the impetus behind the drivers of deforestation and forest degradation. As the international community rallies around REDD, and developed countries and companies are willing to commit substantial amounts to implement the scheme, this books seeks to address whether REDD has the potential to achieve its purported goals.

This is an important resource for academics and students interested in the policy and management aspects of climate change mitigation, environmental policy, international relations, and development studies as well as policy makers involved in the REDD process.

Jessica L. DeShazo is Assistant Professor at California State University at Los Angeles, USA.

Chandra Lal Pandey is a Visiting Professor in School of Education, Kathmandu University, the Institute of Crisis Management and International Relations and Diplomacy Programme at Tribhuvan University, Nepal. He is also a Senior Research Fellow at Southasia Institute of Advanced Studies.

Zachary A. Smith is Regents Professor at Northern Arizona University, USA.

Routledge Studies in Environmental Policy

Why REDD will Fail

Jessica L. DeShazo, Chandra Lal
Pandey and Zachary A. Smith

Routledge
Taylor & Francis Group

LONDON AND NEW YORK

First published 2016
by Routledge
4 Park Square, Milton Park, Abingdon, Oxon OX14 4RN

and by Routledge
605 Third Avenue, New York, NY 10017

Routledge is an imprint of the Taylor & Francis Group, an informa business

British Library Cataloguing-in-Publication Data
A catalogue record for this book is available from the British Library

Library of Congress Cataloging-in-Publication Data
Names: DeShazo, Jessica L., author. | Pandey, Chandra Lal, 1975– , author | Smith, Zachary A. (Zachary Alden), 1953– , author.
Title: Why REDD will fail / Jessica L. DeShazo, Chandra Lal Pandey, and Zachary A. Smith.
Description: New York, NY : Routledge, 2016.
Identifiers: LCCN 2015048210 | ISBN 9780415729260 (hb) | ISBN 9781315851105 (ebook)
Subjects: LCSH: Forest protection—International cooperation. | Forest protection—Economic aspects.
Classification: LCC SD411 .D47 2016 | DDC 333.75/16—dc23
LC record available at http://lccn.loc.gov/2015048210

ISBN: 978-0-415-72926-0 (hbk)
ISBN: 978-1-315-85110-5 (ebk)

Typeset in Times New Roman
by Apex CoVantage, LLC

Jessica:
For the women who raised me.

Chandra:
This book is dedicated to all forest-dependent people and all the endangered species. We believe the forthcoming climate agreement would be a milestone for reducing greenhouse gases and managing forest sustainably.

Zachary:
For Alden and Genevieve.

Contents

1 An introduction to REDD

Forests cover approximately 30 percent of the Earth's land surface, just over 4 billion hectares. Forests may be one of the most important ecosystems on Earth because of the ecological services they provide. These include promoting climate stability, protecting biodiversity and watersheds, providing resources for human consumption, and preventing soil erosion. Forests also protect against salinization of the soil. Salinization leads to desertification, the conversion of arable land into desert-like conditions. Forests are destroyed for many reasons, including for livestock grazing, fuelwood, and the conversion of forestland for agricultural and commercial timber production. All of these things lead to deforestation. It is estimated that over 15 million hectares are lost to deforestation each year, contributing just under 20 percent of all greenhouse gas (GHG) emissions. Deforestation is particularly devastating when it happens in old growth (or primary) forests. Primary forests undisturbed by human activity currently constitute only one-third of the total forested land area. Older trees absorb carbon dioxide more efficiently than do reforested areas.

Natural forests can sustain themselves without any human intervention because they are genetically diverse and self-regulating. Half of all plant and animal species are located in forests, and they are considered to be libraries of information regarding genetic diversity. When deforestation occurs, biodiversity is lost because the habitat for forest species is lost. A forest needs biodiversity to maintain its ecosystem. This genetic diversity in forests allows species to cope with changing environmental factors and thus survive. Depleting biodiversity robs an ecosystem of its ability to adapt to and survive changing environmental conditions.

Climate stability could be the most important service forests provide. Forests are a natural sink, absorbing the GHG carbon dioxide. GHGs trap heat from the sun, thus increasing the Earth's atmospheric temperature. Humans are increasing the amount of GHGs released into the air by the increased burning of fossil fuels, which releases carbon dioxide into the air. Forests convert carbon dioxide to oxygen. However, deforestation has reduced the amount of carbon dioxide that is converted, leaving the gas in the air.

The international community has recognized for several decades that climate change threatens to disrupt many human activities. Agriculture, the viability of ecosystems, species in the oceans and on land, and inhabitants in coastal areas all over the planet are now in jeopardy. Deforestation and forest degradation account for close to 20 percent of the GHGs emitted globally. It is the third leading source of GHG emissions, behind only the energy and industrial sectors (US Environmental Protection Agency, 2015). This degradation takes place through many forms including logging, burning, and removal of forests to create land for farming and other purposes.

In this book we will examine the most important and promising international effort that has been undertaken to deal with GHGs and climate change – the program known as Reducing Emissions from Deforestation and Forest Degradation (REDD) in developing countries. As you will see in the following chapters, the REDD effort is a noble one but is destined to fail. Our aim is not to simply criticize efforts to date but to emphasize the problems with REDD in the hope that modifications can be made that will lead to a better future.

To understand how REDD will fail, it is important to understand the institutional incentives and constraints that operate on the actors that are overseeing and managing the forests as well as the incentives that motivate the non-governmental organizations and corporations that have become the players in the REDD story. These are people and organizations that work in a global economy with global markets for forest resources. The mechanisms that have been established by REDD are well intended and can work on a limited scale. However, unfortunately, the weaknesses of these methods – as detailed in chapter 3 and elsewhere – virtually guarantee that REDD, unless significantly reformed, will not accomplish its objectives in the long term.

We conclude this book with recommendations that we think will greatly improve REDD. These recommendations basically involve much more money – primarily to offset competing demands for forest products and to greatly enhance forest monitoring. Although we feel the suggestions we make for improving REDD will help greatly, we are not sanguine about the chances that REDD will meet its objectives even if our recommendations are adopted. But it is important to understand the legal and institutional weaknesses of any policy before one can begin to make the necessary adjustments in that policy to improve the chances of success. We will begin by providing a brief history of REDD and then an overview of what REDD is and what it hopes to accomplish.

The first major step toward an international effort to reduce GHG emissions was the signing of the United Nations Framework Convention on Climate Change at the Earth Summit in Rio de Janeiro in 1992. Out of this framework came the Conference of Parties (COP). The COP meets to discuss the implementation and progress of policies aimed at reducing global climate change. The seeds of REDD can be traced to Kyoto Protocol in December 1997, where deforestation was identified as a major problem that has to be addressed. That same year the first REDD-type project was formalized – the Noel Kempff Mercado Climate Action Project. Located in northeastern Bolivia this 3.9-million-acre project was funded by a handful of environmental non-governmental organizations and a much larger number of carbon-producing corporations. The Noel Kempff Project was established with a 30-year lifespan.

During the meeting of COP 11 the idea of reducing GHG emissions through the protection of forests was fully realized (Allan & Dauvergne, 2013). The original concept was to reduce the emission of carbon into the atmosphere by protecting forests. Eventually, this evolved into what is now called REDD.

REDD's focus is on the reduction of carbon emissions through reducing the amount of forest that is destroyed and degraded every year. REDD formally started in its current form in 2008. The UN role is to support national efforts and the private sector, and to ensure the involvement of stakeholders in the process of developing and implementing REDD projects.

What is REDD?

Basically, REDD allowed for the commodification of forest resources. Stated another way, REDD moves the carbon sequestration capacity of the forest into the market economy. The program has created a system to quantify and deliver market value for the carbon that is stored in forests. A verified emissions reduction unit represents one ton of carbon dioxide emissions. Corporations can purchase these emissions reduction units to offset their carbon footprint from manufacturing or other activities. Once purchased, carbon credits are freely marketable and may be traded or sold to other carbon emitters (for example, via the International Emissions Trading Association). These are sold as either certified emission reductions or market-verified emission reductions.

Developing countries and the owners of private forestlands can use REDD funds to preserve forested land and prevent it from being deforested or otherwise degraded. Protecting forested lands, and hence maintaining their ability to sequester carbon, is the primary goal of REDD. The ability to understand the diverse threats to forests allows REDD to be a flexible and adaptable instrument to combat these issues. Additionally, it takes into account the capabilities and constraints of the partner countries in order to develop the most efficient programs possible. In its initial framework the United Nations Collaborative Programme on Reducing Emissions from Deforestation and Forest Degradation in Developing Countries states just how different risks to forests can be:

> While the primary cause of deforestation in Latin America was a conversion of forests to large scale permanent agriculture, in Africa deforestation was mainly caused by conversion of forests to small scale permanent agriculture and in Asia there was a mix of direct causes. The underlying causes are often even more intractable, ranging from governance structures, land tenure systems and law enforcement, to market and cultural values of forests, to the rights of indigenous and local communities and benefit sharing mechanisms, to poverty and food production policies. As a result, solutions need to be tailor-made to the environmental and socio-economic conditions of each and every country and their institutional capacity.
>
> (UN-REDD Programme, 2009, p. 2)

REDD is a multilevel system *capable* of addressing the issue of deforestation and GHG emissions as well as local concerns such as those dealing with indigenous populations. REDD's mission includes the sustainable management and conservation of forests, and the improvement of forest carbon stocks. The realization of these goals could make REDD more than just a strategy to protect forests and reduce carbon emissions. It is unclear if these other objectives, in particular incorporating the needs and interests of indigenous people, will play a significant role in REDD in the future.

There are benefits that draw countries to become partners in REDD. One of the main benefits is that it is cost effective inasmuch as developing countries are not required to fund additional infrastructure (Kanowski, McDermott, & Cashore, 2011). While many other policies aimed at reducing carbon and other GHG emissions require either production to be decreased or new technologies to be developed, REDD does not. On its most basic level it requires only that forests be protected and maintained in order to sustain their current carbon stocks. This has appeal for many developing countries that either do not have the money to develop new technologies or do not want to restrict the industrial sectors they host. While developing measures for monitoring does produce some costs to countries, there is funding available to them to assist in the start-up and continuation of measuring and monitoring.

Other benefits that may occur from instituting REDD policies include the protection of biodiversity as well as social benefits such as community engagement. Forests are home to many different species of animals and plants, some of which have not yet been discovered. Not only maintaining but also increasing the forested areas in countries will provide a haven for these species of life to expand and flourish. Social benefits may also be felt throughout the country. Community involvement in these strategies is essential for REDD to work. As a result of their involvement, communities and countries may experience a greater sense of cohesion and stronger governance, which would support individual as well as societal well-being.

As noted above, these benefits may or may not fully develop in the future of REDD. Measurement, Reporting, and Verification (MRV) is the costliest part of REDD implementation. Forests can be certified through Climate, Community, and Biodiversity Standards, and carbon can be measured via Verified Carbon Standards, to get ready for the marketing of credits, but there is still no guarantee that the long-term concerns of indigenous people or the carbon or biodiversity goals will continue to be met with lax MRV. Furthermore, when REDD forests are created with a limited lifespan, like the Noel Kempff Project, then REDD may just be forestalling the enviable. Conservation easements would be a much better approach.

Who is involved in REDD?

The implementation of REDD takes the cooperation of many different partners. These players range from donor countries to international organizations and partner countries and all the way down to local indigenous populations (LIPs). For the sake of simplification the partners involved will be classified into the three different subsets: donors and finance, the UN-REDD Programme, and stakeholders.

Donors and finance

Developing and implementing programs aimed at reducing emissions, along with the measurements needed to verify reductions, costs money. The financial backing needed for the mission of REDD comes from a variety of sources. These sources range from individual countries to international financial institutions such as the World Bank and corporations. Countries such as Denmark, Japan, Luxembourg, Spain, and Norway have all directly invested funds in REDD. In fact, Norway has contributed over US$200 million since 2008, a figure that is more than seven times the amount of the previously mentioned countries combined (Multi-Partner Trust Fund Office, 2015). These funds are deposited in the Multi-Partner Trust Fund and then distributed to the UN-REDD Programme for use in, and distribution to, developing countries. Another financial backer of REDD is the World Bank through the Forest Carbon Partnership Facility (FCPF). The World Bank has a history of supporting forestry projects, although some have not been beneficial to forests. It wasn't until the 1990s that it changed its policies to focus more on forest sustainability and management as opposed to harvesting. The FCPF was started in 2008 and works with the United Nations to implement REDD. Like the Multi-Partner Trust Fund, it receives donations from various countries, and those donations are consolidated into one of two funds. The first is the Readiness Fund, whose purpose is to help developing countries prepare to incorporate REDD strategies into their countries (FCPF, 2015). The Readiness Fund provides financial assistance to countries that need and want help in the planning phases of REDD. This covers topics such as how to maintain and grow forests, how to measure carbon levels, and how to verify that these levels are accurate. These issues must be addressed before REDD can be put in place within a country. The second fund is the Carbon Fund, which aims to pay incentives to developing countries that maintain their forests and the carbon stocks within them. This fund is set up to pilot incentives for countries as well as test and verify how the country is implementing REDD strategies. This is different from payments from developed countries in that this is a testing phase and no offsets can be purchased by developing countries during this time.

The UN-REDD Programme

The UN-REDD Programme is a collaboration between three primary organizations that are able to assist developing countries in the design and implementation of REDD. The first organization is the United Nations Development Programme (UNDP). The UNDP is well suited for such a task as it already works with (and in) developing countries and has an understanding of the challenges and obstacles that will be faced when trying to introduce new programs into these countries. The UNDP works to engage communities and LIPs in developing countries as part of a plan to incorporate all players into the REDD system (UN-REDD Programme, 2011).

The United Nations Environment Programme (UNEP) works with countries to take steps forward toward a green economy and ensures that benefits from REDD are understood and being obtained. The UNEP assists countries in assessing the benefits and trade-offs of REDD. This may include the enhancement of carbon stocks, a change in the levels of biodiversity within forests, and even the possibility of increasing donor support. Trade-offs can be of concern as they take away from one area to give to another. The UNEP assists in making sure that when trade-offs do take place, they do not infringe on the rights of people, and the benefits from the trade-off are greater than any losses. In addition to trade-offs and benefits the UNEP also works with countries to help promote a green economy. The successful management of forests and sustainable development that poses minimal environmental risks support REDD goals as well as the goals of a green economy.

The Food and Agriculture Organization (FAO) takes charge in MRV (UN-REDD Programme, 2011). The FAO considers "forestry initiatives as consistent with food security and poverty reduction" (Araneta-Alana, 2013, p. 577). With forestry monitoring programs that evaluate the environmental as well as economic aspects of forests, the FAO has the capacity and capabilities to guide countries in the measuring and monitoring process needed for REDD to succeed. Together, these three organizations make up the UN-REDD Programme that works to help developing countries implement REDD strategies by providing them with expertise and assistance.

Stakeholders

Each developing country that participates in REDD has an interest and an investment in its strategies; these countries, and the communities and LIPs within them, are stakeholders in REDD. For stakeholders it is important to understand and be a part of REDD, as they are the ones who will feel the greatest impact of REDD. As of 2016 there were 62 partner countries in REDD across Africa, Asia-Pacific, and Latin America and the Caribbean. While not all partner countries have taken on REDD projects, they have each pledged to incorporate the values and strategies of REDD. Within the countries that do take on projects, and even those who have only pledged to incorporate REDD values, are the communities and LIPs who also take on these values and are an important part in the success of REDD. Community involvement is an essential part of making sure that these strategies work. Not only do communities help to implement the strategies, but they are also the ones who will reap the benefits of successful strategies. LIPs can be a benefit and a challenge to REDD. The knowledge of forests that LIPs possess can be a major advantage in developing ways to maintain and protect forests. However, the rights of LIPs must still be protected and incorporated into REDD strategies. The UN-REDD Programme along with the FCPF intend to uphold and comply with the UN Declaration of the Rights of Indigenous Peoples (UN-REDD Programme, 2011).

How does REDD work?

There are two main ways in which REDD works to attain its goals. The first is through direct development of strategies and monitoring systems. The second is through support of existing policies that have been put in place by partner countries and through assistance to countries in the monitoring and reporting of findings. Deciding which role is best depends on the needs of the partner country and its internal capabilities.

The first step is to identify the need to protect a forest. This identification has to come from both the UN-REDD Programme and the partner country. One way to do this is by examining the amount of forested land lost per year and the reasons it is being lost. Once a need is identified, a proposal for REDD inclusion is completed in order to gain financial assistance, if needed, to start the development of strategies. The FCPF provides assistance to countries so that they may develop the plans, budgets, and strategies necessary to implement REDD (FCPF, 2015). The next step taken toward the implementation of REDD is to submit a proposal for review and approval by the Participants Committee (Thompson, Baruah, & Carr, 2011). This committee includes members from donor countries, participant countries, and the FCPF. The submitted proposal must gain approval before any main financing can be distributed to the host country. The criteria employed by the Participants Committee include elements such as potential trade-offs, the engagement and participation of LIPs, sustainability, and measurement and monitoring practices (Thompson, Baruah, & Carr, 2011). While the UN-REDD Programme is able and willing to assist in the development of strategies and monitoring practices, most of the responsibility for such actions is placed on the host country. They are responsible for engaging the community and LIPs, bringing in outside agencies or organizations if need be, and establishing a monitoring and reporting system (UN-REDD Programme, 2009). The emphasis on the host country is important so that the goals of REDD are internalized by the government and society within the host country. One of the most important parts in the process of developing the readiness to move forward with REDD is identifying the stakeholders that need to be involved. Engagement of both communities and LIPs within the context of the strategies that are developed is crucial to its success.

Once proposals have been developed they are then submitted to the UN-REDD Policy Board for review. The Policy Board is made up of partner countries, donor countries, indigenous peoples, civil society, and the three UN organizations (UN-REDD Programme, 2015a). The board's main objective is to review proposals and ensure that they are within the framework of REDD and give direction when needed. The goal of the review is to ensure that the proposal meets all the criteria necessary to enact efficient REDD strategies. It is in the development of these proposals that the experience of the agencies that make up the UN-REDD Programme can be put to use. The UN-REDD Programme may help countries in areas such as assessing the scope of roles, identifying and bringing together stakeholders, and developing measures to monitor forest growth and emissions reductions (UN-REDD Programme, 2009). Each agency within the program has years of experience in the development process and therefore is an asset that can prove extremely useful to host countries who are looking to develop a REDD proposal.

Once a proposal has been approved it can then be put into place and financing can be released to the host country. In order to ensure that the strategies that have been approved are implemented, there has to be a system of monitoring available to both the host country and the UN-REDD Programme; these systems are also outlined in the proposal. MRV and monitoring are used to gauge the success of the proposal. MRV and monitoring may be developed from models used by other countries or may be original in the proposal as long as they can be effective. MRV tools are used to first establish baseline measures of GHG emissions, as well as of forested areas (UN-REDD Programme, 2009). Monitoring of all the variables measured is left to the host country as long as all MRV and monitoring are transparent, accurate, and precise (UN-REDD Programme, 2011). The need for systems of measurement that are transparent is great in order to keep host countries accountable not only to the goals of REDD but also to the UN-REDD Programme, which allocates payments to countries based on their reporting.

The second method that REDD uses to achieve the goal of reduced GHG emissions is to support national policies that are already in place in partner countries. As one example, in the country of Bhutan a minimum of 60 percent of its total area is under forested cover in accordance with the country's constitution (UN-REDD Programme, 2015b). Here REDD may benefit Bhutan by merely offering tools for monitoring of GHG emissions rather than developing strategies to increase forested areas within the country.

REDD is one way to greatly reduce GHG emissions. It offers support to developing countries either through a direct-action plan that includes development of strategies or through support for the efforts of national policies that are already in place. We do not want to diminish the importance of the contribution REDD has made to mitigating carbon in the atmosphere. Clearly REDD has played, and will play, a role in forest management in the future either through providing assistance to developing countries or leading those countries into carbon markets through REDD. That having been said, it is also clear that REDD is a well-intended half step that will ultimately not achieve the goals of its proponents. REDD will fail in this respect. We will deal with the faults surrounding REDD later in the book. In this introductory chapter we will simply introduce the reader to some of the most notable criticisms of the program.

Criticisms

Most of the criticisms REDD receives come from environmental and human rights groups. These groups are also concerned with reducing GHG emissions and doing it in a sustainable way. Their criticisms primarily concern protections for those who live in and off the forest and the environmental side effects of REDD (which we discuss in chapter 3). We would like to make clear at the outset that we understand and agree with the criticisms often leveled by these groups. However, our aim here is not to address those REDD problems but to focus on why REDD will fail to achieve what it claims it will do. Nonetheless, we will summarize the criticisms of those groups here.

One of the biggest criticisms of REDD, and one that leads to other criticisms, is how forests are defined. When the word *forest* is used oftentimes we think of something similar to the Amazon or another rainforest; we think of a variety of trees and other vegetation that provide food and shelter for a plethora of animals and insects. While this concept of a forest is included in the definition used by REDD, so are other concepts of forests. Tree plantations, genetically engineered trees, and clear-cut areas are also included in the definition of forests under REDD. We will cover this in greater detail in chapter 3 of this book.

Communities that depend on forests are also critical of REDD. If the definition of forests has been a source of criticism, the lack of a definition of forest degradation has likewise been criticized. There is no agreed-upon definition for the term *forest degradation*, but working definitions include activities such as shifting cultivation and foraging (Lang, 2009). Communities who have lived in and on the forests for generations with minimal harm to the forests will now be considered part of the problem should a definition that contains this language be adopted. A move to use this language not only would be contrary to a mission of REDD, which is to observe the rights of LIPs, but could also have a negative effect and create strong opposition to REDD within a country. Forest-dependent communities place minimal demands on forest resources, unlike the governments of developed and developing countries.

REDD, as stated earlier, does not address countries' consumption practices but instead focuses on sustainable management of forests and reduction of forest destruction. However, many critics argue that unless the issue of consumption is addressed then REDD will not achieve the desired results. The eventual goal of REDD is that developed countries will pay developing countries to protect and enhance their forests in order to offset carbon emissions. This practice allows developed countries to claim that they are reducing emissions when no actual reduction has taken place (Global Justice Equality Project, 2010). Also, should a developing country adopt REDD and preserve its forests, this does not equate to a reduction in deforestation. While deforestation practices may be reduced or cease altogether in that country, they may be ramped up in another country. This is called leakage and will be discussed in greater detail in the following chapters. Without strong governance in place to support REDD there is no guarantee that deforestation practices will be reduced. Illegal logging operations supported by weak or corrupt governments are contributors to deforestation. Unless these issues are dealt with, critics believe that REDD is incapable of reducing carbon emissions and deforestation.

Moving forward

In chapter 2 we provide further elaboration on some of the topics covered in this chapter, including Kyoto, and a further examination of the operations of REDD. It explains how REDD has evolved from first considering forests as part of climate mitigation to an expanded role that includes much more. We introduce the concept of sustainable forest management and how it relates to REDD. In addition, we outline the key actors involved with REDD.

Chapter 3 provides a more detailed examination of the problems associated with REDD. It is in this chapter that we provide the basis for our argument that ultimately REDD will not accomplish its objectives – and our reasons that REDD will fail. We examine the complications with defining what is a forest. We then move on to the problems with leakage and the push for additionality.

Chapter 4 sheds lights on the locations of REDD projects in Asia, Africa, and Latin America. This chapter provides the details of the direct drivers of deforestation in these three different regions/continents to indicate the reasons forests are being deforested. It shows that in Latin America deforestation and degradation are mainly done for commercial agriculture. In Africa deforestation primarily takes place for subsistence farming, whereas in Asia the reasons for deforestation are a mixture of both. The chapter also points out that these direct drivers of deforestation are connected to indirect drivers such as the economic interests of the actors and the global capitalist economic system.

Chapter 5 discusses the larger international power dynamic at play in REDD. Specifically, it examines how a global capitalist economy drives deforestation. In this chapter we explain how the economies of developing countries are linked to those of developed countries. We then go on to examine the problems with using the private sector to fund REDD and the issues that arise from lack of transparency. Last, the problems of market volatility and the need for permanent funding are addressed.

In chapter 6 we address the strengths and limitations of REDD and make attempts to answer the question: can REDD help developing countries achieve economic growth and mitigate climate change? The chapter demonstrates that REDD may provide some important opportunities to developing and least developed countries but that there are serious concerns that need attention before we can make a considered judgment about REDD's potential success. We contextualize the explanation of institutional constraints, which focuses on protection of the forests in the developing countries and least developed countries for carbon storage but does not help developed countries reduce emissions domestically. We explore the limitations of REDD, in the context of rising demand for global wood products and agricultural goods in rich countries as well as among "pockets of rich" in emerging economies, and monoculture tree plantations that reflect the goals of global capitalism instead of the concerns of global climate change, poverty reduction, and forest protection.

In the concluding chapter of the book we summarize the steps that we feel are necessary to improve REDD.

References

Allan, J. I., & Dauvergne, P. (2013). The global South in environmental negotiations: The politics of coalitions in REDD. *Third World Quarterly, 34*(8), 1307–1322. http://dx.doi.org/10.1080/01436597.2013.831536

Araneta-Alana, N. (2013). The Food and Agriculture Organization as agent of civic environmentalism discourse in the intersect of REDD+, agriculture, forestry, and food security. *Ateneo Law Journal, 58*(3), 577–611.

Forest Carbon Partnership Facility (FCPF). (2015). *The Readiness Fund.* Retrieved from https://www.forestcarbonpartnership.org/readiness-fund-0

Global Justice Equality Project. (2010). *Why REDD is wrong.* Retrieved from http://globaljusticeecology.org/why-redd-is-wrong/

Kanowski, P. J., McDermott, C. L., & Cashore, B. W. (2011). Implementing REDD+: Lessons from analysis of forest governance. *Environmental Science & Policy, 14*(2), 111–117. http://dx.doi.org/10.1016/j.envsci.2010.11.007

Lang, C. (2009). REDD will fail with the current definition of "forest." *REDD Monitor.* Retrieved from http://www.redd-monitor.org/2009/09/08/redd-will-fail-with-the-current-definition-of-forest/

Multi-Partner Trust Fund Office. (2015). *UN REDD programme fund.* Retrieved from http://mptf.undp.org/factsheet/fund/CCF00

Thompson, M. C., Baruah, M., & Carr, E. R. (2011). Seeing REDD as a project of environmental governance. *Environmental Science & Policy, 14*(2), 100–110. http://dx.doi.org/10.1016/j.envsci.2010.11.006

United Nations Collaborative Programme on Reducing Emissions from Deforestation and Forest Degradation in Developing Countries (UN-REDD Programme). (2009). *Framework document.* Retrieved from http://www.unredd.net/index.php?view=document&alias=4-un-redd-programme-framework-document-20-june-2008-4&category_slug=foundation-documents-88&layout=default&option=com_docman&Itemid=134

United Nations Collaborative Programme on Reducing Emissions from Deforestation and Forest Degradation in Developing Countries (UN-REDD Programme).

(2011). *The UN-REDD programme strategy.* Retrieved from http://www.unredd.
org/Portals/15/documents/publications/UNREDD_FrameworkDocument.pdf

United Nations Collaborative Programme on Reducing Emissions from Deforestation and Forest Degradation in Developing Countries (UN-REDD Programme).
(2015a). *Regions and countries overview.* Retrieved from http://www.unredd.net/
index.php?option=com_unregions&view=overview&Itemid=495

United Nations Collaborative Programme on Reducing Emissions from Deforestation and Forest Degradation in Developing Countries (UN-REDD Programme).
(2015b). *Two-pager of REDD national strategy/action plan: Bhutan.* Retrieved from
http://www.unredd.net/index.php?view=document&alias=14491-two-pager-of-
redd-national-strategyaction-plan-bhutan&category_slug=asia-pacific-un-redd-
regional-exchange-event-on-redd-national-strategy-and-action-plan-july-2015&
layout=default&option=com_docman&Itemid=134

US Environmental Protection Agency. (2015). *Global greenhouse gas emissions
data.* Retrieved from http://www3.epa.gov/climatechange/ghgemissions/global.
html

2 The evolution of REDD

In human history, forests were once seen as an inexhaustible resource. Reducing Emissions from Deforestation and Forest Degradation (REDD), both as an approach to climate mitigation and as a development tool, has evolved from previous policies of the United Nations and the World Bank. The management of forests after considerable destruction has deep historical roots. Industrialized countries have a pattern of over-utilizing this natural resource. Before we can understand REDD and its evolution, we must first address the development of scientific forestry, which began in developed European countries and the United States. Before scientific management, the wasting of forest resources, such as timber, was not identified as a problem in developed countries, nor were the severe ecological harms that result from clear cutting. In this chapter we explore the development of scientific management of forests as it relates to the evolution of REDD. We then go on to discuss how REDD evolved, from its first mention to the international scheme that has developed. Last, we provide an overview of the main actors involved with REDD and begin our discussion on how this scheme is funded.

Forest regulation in developed countries

Forest regulation in developed countries centers on the use of scientific management. This type of management applies scientific knowledge to the control of forest resources as well as transforms the political institutions that oversee the administration of those resources. The logic of science is used to shift the focus of institutions and the way they operate in order to align with the goals of managing natural resources to achieve a sustained supply.

Scientific management

Scientific management was in full swing by the late 19th century. It centered on the skills of technical experts to manage the various problems faced by society (Nelson, 1995). These technical experts were expected to be an elite group that was removed from politics and relied solely on scientific information when making decisions (Nelson, 1995). Scientific management sought to supply objective answers to social problems that were often based on competing values. In this case, the problem was a shortage of forests and timber. Scientific management largely meant a sustained yield of forest resources. Before scientific management, the focus was on preservation of forests.

Scientific management of forests first began in developed countries. Its roots can be traced back to Germany in the 19th century. Access to forests was often limited, but it was for economic and colonial interests rather than to protect the environment. In the United States during the colonial period, forests were conserved for use by the British Crown only. Britain wanted to keep all trees over a particular diameter and height for ship building (Ise, 1920). In 1701 the governor of New York made a suggestion that for every tree cut down, four or five should be planted. It was over 40 years before the independent United States began to issue regulations regarding forests. Beginning in 1831 timber was not allowed to be taken from public lands (Steen, 1976). However, Steen (1976) points out that for the first century of the newly minted United States, forests, or timberland, were not acknowledged in legislation. By 1874 something had to be done. The secretary of the interior, Columbus Delano, noted that timber on public lands was being depleted (Steen, 1976). The Timber Culture Act of 1873 was the first of its kind to recognize timberland. It is Gifford Pinchot who is best known for making an impact on forestry practices in the United States. Pinchot was trained in Germany in the scientific management of forests. He also studied forestry in France, Switzerland, and Austria (Pennsylvania Historical and Museum Commission, n.d.). The first country to have a formal educational curriculum for forestry was Germany, with France following shortly after (Farrell et al., 2000). These countries, especially Germany, effectively led the way in scientific management and preservation of forests.

During the Enclosure period, trees became a serious economic source rather than just a public good. Trees that had a high monetary value became timber, and the rest was considered worthless and not preserved. This trend of preserving only valuable species led to a loss of biodiversity. Germany was the first to develop scientific management of forests during the late 18th century (Scott, 1998). Scientific management gave way to further enclosures, which omitted them from being part of the commons (Humphreys, 2006). Before scientific management, forests were assumed to be limitless in terms of timber, and countries did not focus on preserving them. Forests and their connection to watersheds were understood; however, timber was the only economic commodity derived from forests early on. Carbon and other non-timber forest products were not recognized until much later. Scientific management and regulation of forests in Germany and Austria largely resulted from mining. A large supply of timber was needed to build and operate mines. This caused widespread destruction, and thus scientific management was used to maintain the supply of timber for mining operations. The Germans used the term *Nachhaltigkeitsprinzip* to refer to sustainability in forestry (Wiersum, 1995).

The impact of scientific management today

Early forestry regulation was based on the use of timber. Scientific management of forests to achieve sustainable forestry now has a modern-day translation to sustained yield and multiple use. *Sustained yield* means maintaining a constant supply of timber and other forest resources. *Multiple use* refers to moving beyond valuing forests in terms of timber supply only and allowing other human-valued products and services to be derived from a forest (Wiersum, 1995). Wiersum (1995, p. 322) concludes that sustainable forestry "has been defined as the need to maintain the productive capacity and ecological integrity of forests . . . and to arrange for such external conditions that forest managers are able to sustain these management practices."

As we show later in the chapter, REDD changes how forests are used, or, rather, not used. REDD is about maintaining carbon sequestration capacity or increasing that capacity along with reducing carbon emissions in order to mitigate climate change. It is heavily embedded in the concept of scientific management, but instead of timber, the forests are used for carbon sequestration and storage. Just as forests were preserved for the most powerful countries during colonialism, the same is happening today with REDD. It is a new form of colonialization. This topic is discussed further in chapter 5.

Noordwijk Declaration on Climate Change

So how did we get from forests as sources of timber to a focus on forests as a source of carbon sequestration and storage? One of the first instances of international recognition of carbon dioxide as being harmful took place with the Noordwijk Declaration. The Noordwijk Declaration on Climate Change was the result of a meeting that took place in 1989 in Noordwijk, the Netherlands. At this conference, over 60 countries and nearly a dozen international organizations recognized the need to stabilize carbon dioxide and other greenhouse gas (GHG) emissions (Information Unit on Climate Change [IUCC], 1993a). The conference filled in some gaps in the 1987 Montreal Protocol, which focused more on the regulation of chlorofluorocarbons and halons. The goal of the Montreal Protocol was to prevent human-caused damage to the ozone layer through the use of those chemicals (IUCC, 1993b). The Noordwijk Declaration proclaimed that stabilization of carbon dioxide should be achieved by 2000 for industrialized countries. Unlike for REDD, the focus was not on the global South since industrialized countries in the global North were the major emitters. As we now know, such stabilization did not occur. In fact, it was not until much later, in 2009, that the United States nationally declared carbon dioxide to be a pollutant (US Environmental Protection Agency, 2009). There are two reasons why the Noordwijk conference is significant. First, carbon dioxide became an international concern that was recognized as needing to be stabilized. Second, climate change was recognized as a common concern. In addition, the participants stressed that more research on climate change was needed and that there should be financial assistance and technology transfers to developing countries. The weakness of the declaration is that states were left to address the issue according to their own choices (IUCC, 1993a).

Kyoto Protocol

The first comprehensive attempt to address climate change and GHG emissions was the Kyoto Protocol, but it did not see the role that forests could play in such efforts. Whereas the Noordwijk Declaration recognized the harm caused by GHG emissions and called for more research, the Kyoto Protocol was more about taking action as a result of the earlier research findings. The history of the Kyoto Protocol begins with the Rio Earth Summit that was held in Rio de Janeiro, Brazil, in 1992. During this conference, the United Nations Framework Convention on Climate Change (UNFCCC) was negotiated. The Kyoto Protocol comes directly out of the UNFCCC. One hundred sixty-one countries came together in Kyoto, Japan, in December 1997 in an effort to reach a multilateral agreement to reduce the threat of climate change while also minimizing the impact such efforts would have on any one country's or region's economic growth (Smith, 2013). The participants in the Kyoto Protocol are mostly developed countries. It was the first international initiative of its kind to commit to addressing global climate change, but considering impacts on economic growth as another concern.

The Kyoto Protocol's focus was on limiting GHGs. REDD differs from the Kyoto Protocol by focusing on carbon, just one of the GHGs that cause climate change. At this time, the UNFCCC did include forests as part of the effort to mitigate climate change. Forests were included only during the first commitment period of the Kyoto Protocol as part of the Clean Development Mechanism. The Marrakesh Accords in 2001 further stipulated that only afforestation and reforestation activities would be considered part of the Clean Development Mechanism that is part of the Kyoto Protocol (International Union of Concerned Scientists, n.d.). From 1990 to 2005, it is estimated that the average rate of deforestation was 13 million hectares annually (United Nations Collaborative Programme on Reducing Emissions from Deforestation and Forest Degradation in Developing Countries [UN-REDD Programme], 2008b). With the Kyoto Protocol set to expire in 2012, countries worked together to find another mechanism to address climate change that would also assist with helping poorer countries to develop. This effort and the desire to help poorer countries develop was the seed for REDD.

The Noel Kempff Mercado Climate Action Project

The Noel Kempff Mercado Climate Action Project, named after a renowned Bolivian biologist and environmentalist, was created in 1997. It is considered to be the earliest REDD-type project. The Noel Kempff project is a joint effort between the Nature Conservancy and Fundación Amigos de la Naturaleza (Friends of Nature Foundation). The project is in the northeastern part of Bolivia along the Brazilian border. Its financing comes from a mixture of sources: the Bolivian government, the Nature Conservancy (a non-governmental organization), and three corporations. The area is home to a vast number of plant and animal species. Prior to the creation of the project, the area was over-used for logging, ranching, and farming. Roughly US$1.6 million was used to terminate logging rights and turn it into a park. The projected is expected to mitigate an estimated 5.8 million tons of carbon dioxide over a 30-year period. This will be accomplished through the prevention of land conversion to logging and agricultural uses (The Nature Conservancy, 2015).

In 2009 Greenpeace released a report about the problems with the Noel Kempff project. The problems surround the data that are being provided. Leakage has been reported to the UNFCCC and the US Congress at about 15 percent, but some reports have estimated leakage to be as high as 60 percent. Also, the project was initially sold as a way to mitigate much more carbon, up to 55 million tons (Densham et al., 2009).

RED to REDD to REDD Plus

Compensating countries for tropical forest conservation was an idea raised during the meeting in Kyoto; however, it did not seriously become part of the international agenda to address climate change until the Coalition for Rainforest Nations formed in 2005. The Coalition for Rainforest Nations presented a proposal at the Conference of Parties (COP) 11 meeting in

Montreal, Canada, titled "Reducing Emissions from Deforestation in Developing Countries: Approaches to Stimulate Action." This was the first stage, and it is referred to as RED, based on the first four words in the title of the proposal. This report is significant because the COP is the supreme decision-making body within the UNFCCC. The UNFCCC was formed in 1992 out of a meeting held in Rio de Janeiro, Brazil, but the COP did not begin meeting until 1995. They hold regular meetings, and every country that is part of the convention is represented in the COP. The COP usually meets annually. When the Coalition for Rainforest Nations made it onto the COP's agenda, they were able to get the attention of major countries and key players in the fight against climate change.

Two years later, during COP 13 in Bali, Indonesia, in 2007, the Bali Action Plan was developed. It was here that REDD as a serious plan for mitigating climate change was born. The Bali Action Plan called for "policy approaches and positive incentives on issues relating to reducing emissions from deforestation and forest degradation in developing countries [REDD], and the role of conservation, sustainable management of forests and enhancement of forest carbon stock in developing countries" (UNFCCC, 2007). Countries agreed to increase forest resilience and conserve forest stocks through payments for ecosystem services, namely, carbon sequestration, for endangered forests in developing countries. What began as an initiative to address deforestation when first presented in Montreal grew to encompass forest degradation in Bali. Conservation and sustainable management were added as well. Thus, the initiative went from being RED to REDD. The meeting in Bali, just like the meeting in Kyoto, is part of the UNFCCC.

At the COP 14 in Poznan in December 2008, the concept of REDD Plus was first introduced. It was at this meeting that some countries insisted that actions such as conservation, sustainable management of forests, and enhancement of forest carbon stocks be given the same level of priority in the negotiations as both deforestation and forest degradation. These actions were mentioned at COP 11, but they were secondary. After much consideration and talk about the role of forests in mitigating climate change, the first international institution dedicated to the role of forests in mitigation efforts and developing countries was born. The United Nations officially launched its REDD program in 2008. The three UN agencies involved with REDD are the Food and Agriculture Organization, the United Nations Development Programme, and the United Nations Environment Programme. The UN-REDD Programme is governed by a Policy Board that makes decisions about which countries can participate and whether or not REDD activities are approved. Interested country participants must first undergo an approval process to participate within their own government. Once that is done, they must get the approval of their UN resident coordinator. If that approval is gained, the application goes to the Secretariat, which makes a recommendation to the Policy Board about either accepting the application or requesting a resubmission. The Policy Board makes the final decision to either approve the entire program budget, approve part of the budget, or request a resubmission (UN-REDD Programme, 2014).

REDD grew and gained support during the Copenhagen Climate Change Conference in 2009. This was the 15th COP in Copenhagen. At this time REDD Plus became another option to address climate change (The Forests Dialogue, 2010). REDD Plus did not replace REDD. Instead, countries participate in either REDD or REDD Plus activities. REDD Plus differs from REDD because it has the added components of conservation, sustainable forest management, and forest carbon stock enhancement.

The next two COP meetings created mostly minor changes to REDD. At COP 16, in December 2010, REDD became an important part of the Cancun Agreements, in the Outcome of Ad Hoc Working Group on Long-Term Cooperative Action under the Convention. Paragraph 70 of the outcome describes REDD as having multiple goals. These goals are to reduce emissions from deforestation and forest degradation, conserve forest carbon stocks, manage forests sustainably, and enhance forest carbon stocks (UNFCCC, 2011). COP 17 took place in Durban in 2011. It was mostly about financing, safeguards, and reference levels. From this meeting came the Durban Platform for Enhanced Action. The parties also agreed on a second commitment period for the Kyoto Protocol (UNFCCC, 2014b). The participants agreed that results-based financing could come from an array of sources, and that market-based approaches could be used to finance the achievement of desired results. The parties did not clarify what they meant by market-based approaches. Developing countries were supposed to periodically report on how social and environmental safeguards were being addressed, but no information about the amount of detail that was required was given. More information about this would come from COP 18 (UNFCCC, 2012).

COP 18 took place in Doha in 2012. Measurement, Reporting, and Verification of carbon emissions reductions and increased carbon sequestration and storage capacity were the main focus of this meeting. Discussions on Measurement, Reporting, and Verification were begun, but final decisions were delayed until COP 19 in 2013. The issue of verification turned out to be the most difficult one. There was a divide over using two different methods: third-party verifiers or that used for international consultation and analysis for nationally appropriate mitigation actions. There was also much discussion about how to raise the necessary finances for REDD Plus projects. Among the items discussed was the creation of a new institution for REDD Plus and subnational approaches to results-based financing. Since the parties could not reach a decision on verification, they were also unable to finalize a decision on results-based financing, and a work program on the issue was created instead. Finally, draft decisions would be created through a series of workshops and finalized at COP 19 on the following topics: the creation of a new REDD Plus institution, incentives for non-carbon benefits, the creation of a fund for joint adaptation/mitigation actions, and the issue of subnational approaches for results-based payments (UNFCCC, 2013).

At the COP 19 in Warsaw, some advances were made in the safeguards and overall structure of REDD Plus. There are six key areas that were addressed and moved forward at COP 19: financing, transparency and safeguards, monitoring, verification, institutional arrangements, and drivers of deforestation. It was reinforced that financing should be results based, and that developing countries should seek funding from entities such as the Green Climate Fund. Existing funding agencies were asked to follow suit and streamline their processes and rules to match the UNFCCC. The Green Climate Fund was created as part of the UNFCCC. It is the financial branch of the organization. It functions under the guidance of the COP. As for transparency, it was agreed that the UNFCCC website would house an information hub for things such as REDD activities, technical reports, financing, and national action plans. In addition, countries are required to create a full assessment report for how all of the safeguards are being met in their national action plans. The Warsaw Framework made it mandatory for all countries to have a national system in place for monitoring their forests. It also outlines exactly what should be monitored and how. Verification of emissions reductions below an established baseline will occur at the international level. The information will be made publicly available. Countries are encouraged to create national REDD agencies to receive REDD funding and implement the national action plans. This encouragement responded to vagueness about which agency is responsible for REDD activities in the different countries. All entities involved in REDD are encouraged to actively work toward decreasing the drivers of deforestation. One major shortcoming is that those drivers were not defined at this meeting (World Resources Institute, 2013).

When examining the development of REDD, we see that international agreements take a lot of time to develop, from first bringing forth the idea to laying out how it will be implemented. Many stakeholders must be brought to the table, and a considerable amount of research must be done in order to make informed decisions. All of this usually occurs before any agreement is fully implemented and is the reason why REDD has occurred in phases. The UN-REDD Programme began with nine pilot countries in Africa, Asia-Pacific, and Latin America and the Caribbean. Its mission is "to support countries' efforts to reduce emissions from deforestation and

Table 2.1 Summary of Changes from RED to REDD Plus

RED (Reducing Emissions from Deforestation)	The scheme's focus is only on forests that are being cut down and contributing to the release of carbon dioxide.
REDD (Reducing Emissions from Deforestation and Forest Degradation)	The concept of forests that are being degraded, not necessarily cut down, is now part of the focus. Degradation is a decrease in the quality of the forest. There is no single agreed-upon definition for forest degradation.
REDD Plus	Both sustainable management and conservation of biodiversity are added to the scheme.

forest degradation through national REDD strategies that transform their forest sectors so as to contribute to human well-being and meet climate change mitigation and adaptation aspirations" (UN-REDD Programme, 2011). Since the beginning of the pilot program, more countries have been added. Currently, there are roughly 50 countries participating in REDD readiness activities.

At this point countries are receiving money in the readiness phase to create national REDD strategies. Then, once these strategies are being implemented, countries can receive money based on the amount of carbon their forests are sinking or the emissions reductions they achieve. These are results-based payments. Ultimately, REDD is a type of payment for environmental services. Countries are compensated for avoiding deforestation and forest degradation as well as increasing their carbon sequestration capacity through reforestation and afforestation.

Table 2.1 provides a summary of the main environmental developments in the evolution of REDD.

Main actors

So far, we have discussed how REDD has evolved. This evolution occurred mostly through the United Nations. There are other major international organizations and countries involved with REDD. Now we turn to discussing each of the institutions and countries. They are considered the key players in REDD.

The United Nations

The United Nations was one of the first institutions to become involved. It was through this organization that the use of forests to help mitigate climate change began to be addressed. This was when the program was called RED (Reducing Emissions from Deforestation). It was meant for countries with high rates of deforestation, and forest degradation and biodiversity were not yet part of the program. The United Nations launched its UN-REDD Programme in 2008. The UN-REDD Programme began slowly with pilot countries and has expanded greatly over time. Its main focus is on building capacity and assisting with technical expertise (UN-REDD Programme, 2008a).

The Green Climate Fund is the financial branch of the UNFCCC; it provides money to developing countries to support efforts to mitigate climate change (UNFCCC, 2014a). The governance of the fund is done through a board of 24 members. Half are from developed countries, and the other half are from developing countries. In addition, the board has a gender balance. Before someone can be a member of the board of directors, they must have knowledge and experience with both climate change and development finance. The board of directors for the Green Climate Fund functions independently but under the guidance of the COP. The board meets three times a year (Green Climate Fund, 2015). Overall, the Green Climate Fund is mandated to take a country-driven approach when making decisions (Schalatek, Nakhooda, & Watson, 2014). The Green Climated Fund works toward consensus-based decisions between developed and developing countries. It is supposed to provide equal funding for both adapting to climate change and mitigating climate change. Most countries that contribute to the fund are doing so in the form of grants, but France is channeling loan money (Schalatek, Nakhooda, & Watson, 2014). The fund distributes support for capacity building to prepare for implementing REDD Plus. It is still working out a results management framework and the necessary performance indicators (Schalatek, Nakhooda, & Watson, 2014).

The World Bank

The World Bank was created toward the end of World War II by both the United States and Britain with the purpose of being a facilitator of postwar reconstruction and development (World Bank, 2015). The main focus during that period was on rebuilding infrastructure that had been destroyed by the war. Over time, its mission has evolved to focus on poverty alleviation. This newer mission that is centered on poverty alleviation fits with one of the goals of REDD, to help developing countries develop. Today, the World Bank is a large, complex organization consisting of several different agencies, units, and funds.

Many agencies within the World Bank are involved with REDD, for example, the Carbon Finance Unit and the Forest Carbon Partnership Facility (FCPF). The World Bank is involved in providing both funds for capacity building and performance-based payments. The different agencies within the World Bank have divided REDD into three different phases (CIF, 2014). Phase 1 concerns "readiness activities" to help countries prepare for implementing REDD Plus. Phase 2 concerns gathering of investments for REDD implementation. Phase 3 is performance-based payments when countries are fully implementing REDD (CIF, 2014).

The World Bank has been lending money for forestry projects since the 1950s, but at that time it was mostly to support paper mills. Chile received a US$20 million loan, and Bangladesh a US$4.2 million loan, both to support paper mill projects (Hajjar & Innes, 2009). Support for the extraction of timber from forests lasted until 1978. The World Bank also supported the establishment of tree plantations. The first comprehensive World Bank policy about forestry was in 1978. This policy was concerned with the ecological functions of forests and their importance to the agricultural sector. However, it focused on afforestation and reforestation in their importance for rural development rather than conservation or scientific management (Hajjar & Innes, 2009). Furthermore, the World Bank focused on settling tropical forests and clearing valuable species of wood while replanting them with fast-growing tree species that could be used for fuelwood (Hajjar & Innes, 2009). These loans are consistent with the original economic development orientation of the World Bank.

By the 1990s the World Bank had shifted its stance on forests when it began to uphold the preservation of forests. Another change occurred in 2002, when the World Bank finally began to focus on sustainable forest management. It also maintained its focus on using forests to reduce poverty while increasing economic development and protecting the environmental services that forests provide, that is, mitigation of climate change (Hajjar & Innes, 2009). The 2002 forest policy provided the foundation for the integral role the World Bank plays in REDD. The World Bank has been involved with mitigating climate change through a carbon market. According to a World Bank report, "The carbon market is an opportunity . . . to contribute to sustainable development by bringing new public and private funding . . . to developing countries" (Linacre, Ambrosi, & Kossoy, 2011). Currently, the World Bank represents only a fraction of the overall carbon market.

The main agency that is housed within the World Bank that is involved with REDD is the FCPF. It was created in 2008. The FCPF and the UN-REDD Programme are the two largest multilateral programs involved with helping countries to prepare for REDD. It works with the UN-REDD Programme to coordinate efforts aimed at REDD capacity building and technical expertise. The FCPF has two funds: the Readiness Fund and the Carbon Fund. The Readiness Fund is used for what its name suggests, to help countries get ready for implementing REDD. This includes assistance with building both technical and institutional capacity. Many countries do not have the technology or policies and organizations needed to begin implementing REDD. The Carbon Fund is used for performance-based payments, which are actual reductions in emissions from deforestation and forest degradation (FCPF, 2015). There are countries that are participating in both funds, but the Carbon Fund has only five pilot countries.

The Forest Investment Program (FIP) within the World Bank is also involved in REDD. The FIP is part of the Climate Investment Fund within the World Bank. It is a joint partnership of the African Development Bank, the Asian Development Bank, the European Bank for Reconstruction and Development, the Inter-American Development Bank, and the World Bank. The program focuses on REDD and the protection of carbon reservoirs. The FIP is mainly concerned with REDD once it has been implemented and with the reduction of pressures on forests through such means as alternative livelihoods and poverty alleviation (CIF, 2014). However, it does have some funding for preparation activities. It is meant to be a bridge between preparation for REDD and performance-based payments (CIF, 2014). The FIP seeks both public and private sector investments.

The Global Environment Facility

The Global Environment Facility (GEF) is focused on global environmental issues. The facility began in 1991 as a pilot program under the World Bank (GEF, 2013). However, three years later it was established as a separate institution with the World Bank serving as its trustee. The GEF largely serves as a funding mechanism for different international environmental conventions. One of those concerns the role of forests in mitigating climate change, and it works in the area of REDD preparations. It funds pilot projects for what is referred to as SFM/REDD+ (Sustainable Forest Management/REDD Plus) and focuses on cooperation between the public and private sectors. Unlike the other organizations, the GEF does not just focus on conservation. It also focuses on the sustainable management and use of forests and their resources (GEF, 2013). This is important because many less developed countries rely heavily on forest resources, and cutting those off can be detrimental to these countries. This topic is further discussed and illustrated in chapters 5 and 6. In addition to international organizations, a number of other REDD activities have been taking place between individual countries.

Germany

Germany's REDD Early Movers Programme is for countries that have taken independent action to mitigate climate change (The REDD desk, 2016). It is meant to reward those countries that began early efforts to mitigate climate change and to strengthen performance-based payments for emissions reductions (German Federal Ministry for Economic Cooperation and Development). So far, it has only focused on Brazil, Colombia, and Ecuador. The program defines "early movers" as countries that have already made significant progress in both institutional and technical capacity or already have large-scale conservation programs being implemented (German Federal Ministry for Economic Cooperation and Development). This program is different because it specifically does not focus on building capacity, and supports those countries that did not rely on the United Nations or World Bank as they took their first steps. However, it does provide technical and policy advice. The program pays much attention to benefit sharing with sectors that drive deforestation, such as agriculture and livestock breeding. It is also concerned with providing benefits to the indigenous communities that have conserved the forests and rely on them for their livelihoods (German Federal Ministry for Economic Cooperation and Development). The overarching goal of the program is to provide financing for those countries until a more permanent financing solution can be found by the United Nations and World Bank.

Norway

Norway's International Forest and Climate Initiative began in 2007. The initiative is meant to support the reduction of GHG emissions in developing countries as well as conservation of forest carbon stocks, sustainable management of forests, and enhancement of forest carbon stocks. The program supports REDD efforts. It follows the UN-REDD Programme's guidelines for REDD. However, the country provides money to the REDD participants directly (Norway Ministry of Environment and Climate, 2015). Norway's funds are mostly directed toward Brazil and Indonesia. Indonesia entered into an agreement for up to US$1 billion for REDD activities (Edwards, Koh, & Laurance, 2012). Norway also has agreements with Guyana, Mexico, and Tanzania.

Partner countries

Partner countries are those countries that are implementing REDD and are not donor countries. These countries are not industrialized and are located in the global South. The partner countries are located in predominantly tropical and subtropical areas of Africa, Asia-Pacific, and Latin America. They are also referred to as REDD country participants. In order to participate, the country needs to have a large percentage of its land in forests and a rather high level of deforestation and/or forest degradation. This allows for more additionality, or environmental benefits beyond a standard business-as-usual scenario. As of 2015 there are over 60 partner countries in three different regions of the world: Africa, Latin America and the Caribbean, and Asia-Pacific. Tables 2.2 and 2.3 list the partner countries for the UN-REDD

Programme and the FCPF. As you can see, there is much overlap between the participants in these two programs.

The information in table 2.2 is taken from the UN-REDD Programme list of partner countries.

The information in table 2.3 is taken from the FCPF list of REDD Plus countries.

It is important to keep in mind that these countries are in various phases of participation with REDD. Some have only initiated the process of gaining

Table 2.2 UN-REDD Partner Countries

Africa	Asia-Pacific	Latin American and the Caribbean
Benin	Bangladesh	Argentina
Burkina Faso	Bhutan	Bolivia
Cameroon	Cambodia	Chile
Central African Republic	Fiji	Colombia
Chad	India	Costa Rica
Congo	Indonesia	Dominican Republic
Cote d'Ivoire	Lao People's Democratic Republic	Ecuador
Democratic Republic of the Congo	Malaysia	El Salvador
Equatorial Guinea	Mongolia	Guatemala
Ethiopia	Myanmar	Guyana
Gabon	Nepal	Honduras
Ghana	Pakistan	Jamaica
Guinea (Republic of)	Papua New Guinea	Mexico
Guinea Bissau	Philippines	Panama
Kenya	Samoa	Paraguay
Liberia	Solomon Islands	Peru
Madagascar	Sri Lanka	Suriname
Malawi	Vanuatu	
Morocco	Vietnam	
Nigeria		
South Sudan		
Sudan		
Tanzania		
Togo		
Tunisia		
Uganda		
Zambia		
Zimbabwe		

Table 2.3 Forest Carbon Partnership Facility Partner Countries

Africa	Asia-Pacific	Latin American and the Caribbean
Burkina Faso	Bhutan	Argentina
Cameroon	Cambodia	Belize
Central African Republic	Fiji	Bolivia
Cote d'Ivoire	Indonesia	Chile
Democratic Republic of the Congo	Lao People's Democratic Republic	Colombia
Ethiopia	Nepal	Costa Rica
Gabon	Pakistan	Dominican Republic
Ghana	Papua New Guinea	El Salvador
Kenya	Thailand	Guatemala
Liberia	Vanuatu	Guyana
Madagascar	Vietnam	Honduras
Mozambique		Mexico
Nigeria		Nicaragua
Republic of the Congo		Panama
Sudan		Paraguay
Tanzania		Peru
Togo		Suriname
Uganda		Uruguay

approval to participate, while others are moving much closer to full implementation of REDD projects and results-based financing. In chapter 4 we take a closer look at some of the countries that are further along in implementing REDD.

Funding REDD

As of this writing, mostly readiness activities are being funded. No country has begun full implementation of REDD (or REDD Plus). REDD activities are expected to mainly be funded through grants that are results based and the carbon market. Readiness activities are being financed through arrangements with the FCPF and the UN-REDD Programme. It is also anticipated that the World Bank and United Nations will continue to fund second-phase activities as well. The carbon market is expected to be used during the final phase of REDD when projects begin to generate emissions reduction credits. Even though REDD is only in the readiness phase, REDD projects are the fastest growing sector of the carbon market. From 2009 to 2010, REDD's market share grew over 500 percent (Linacre, Ambrosi, & Kossoy, 2011, p. 54). REDD funding is covered in more detail in chapter 5.

Conclusion

REDD schemes are drastically different from initial efforts to curb defor-estation or mitigate climate change. REDD schemes seek to slow both deforestation and forest degradation by paying countries to maintain their current forests and/or reforest degraded areas as well as slow land uses that deplete or degrade forests. Moreover, they target developing countries with the promise of helping them to grow economically without relying on forests. This economic growth is called sustainable development. At the same time, developed countries are not required to slow their emissions of GHGs. Recall that GHG emissions from deforestation and forest degrada-tion account for only 20 percent of all GHG emissions. While this is the second-largest category, the largest category of emissions comes from the energy sector, which accounts for 25.9 percent (Intergovernmental Panel on Climate Change, 2008). Although there have been many efforts to con-serve forests, and REDD would seem the most promising, to date they have proven less than satisfactory. In the next chapter we will examine the spe-cific weaknesses of REDD and the reasons we feel that ultimately it will fail to meet its carbon sequestration and forest preservation goals.

References

Climate Investment Fund (CIF). (2014). *Linkages between REDD+ Readiness and the Forest Investment Program*. Retrieved from http://climateinvestmentfunds. org/cif/node/17292

Densham, A., Czebiniak, R., Kessler, D., & Skar, R. (2009). Carbon scam: Noel Kempff Climate Action Project and the push for subnational forest offsets. *Green-peace International*. Retrieved from http://www.greenpeace.org/international/en/ publications/reports/carbon-scam-noel-kempff-carbo/

Deutsche Gesellschaft fur Internationale Zusammenarbit. (n.d.) *REDD Early Mov-ers*. Retrieved from https://www.giz.de/en/worldwide/33356.html

Edwards, D. P., Koh, L. P., & Laurance, W. F. (2012). Indonesia's REDD pact: Saving imperiled forests or business as usual? *Biological Conservation, 151*(1), 41–44. http://dx.doi.org/10.1016/j.biocon.2011.10.028

Farrell, E. P., Fuhrer, E., Ryan, D., Andersson, F., Huttl, R., & Piussi, P. (2000). Euro-pean forest ecosystems: Building the future on the legacy of the past. *Forest Ecology and Management, 132*(1), 5–20. http://dx.doi.org/10.1016/S0378-1127(00)00375-3

Forest Carbon Partnership Facility (FCPF). (2015). *The Carbon Fund*. Retrieved from https://www.forestcarbonpartnership.org/carbon-fund-0

The Forests Dialogue. (2010). Investing in REDD-plus. *TFD Review*. Retrieved from http://theforestsdialogue.org/publication/investing-redd-plus

Global Environment Facility (GEF). (2013). *What is the GEF*. Retrieved from https://www.thegef.org/gef/whatisgef

Green Climate Fund. (2015). *Overview*. Retrieved from http://www.greenclimate. fund/boardroom/the-board

Hajjar, R., & Innes, J. L. (2009). The evolution of the World Bank's policy towards forestry: Push or pull? *International Forestry Review, 11*(1), 27–37. http://dx.doi.org/10.1505/ifor.11.1.27

Humphreys, D. (2006). *Logjam: Deforestation and the crisis of global governance*. London: Earthscan.

Information Unit on Climate Change (IUCC) of the United Nations Environment Programme. (1993a). *The Noordwijk Declaration on Climate Change*. Retrieved from http://unfccc.int/resource/ccsites/senegal/fact/fs218.htm

Information Unit on Climate Change (IUCC) of the United Nations Environment Programme. (1993b). *Phasing out CFCs: The Vienna Convention and its Montreal Protocol*. Retrieved from http://unfccc.int/resource/ccsites/senegal/fact/fs224.htm

Intergovernmental Panel on Climate Change. (2008). Global anthropogenic GHG emissions. In *Climate Change Synthesis Report: 2007*. Retrieved from http://www.ipcc.ch/publications_and_data/ar4/syr/en/contents.html

International Union for Conservation of Nature. (n.d.). *REDD-plus explained*. Retrieved from http://www.iucn.org/about/work/programmes/forest/fp_our_work/fp_our_work_thematic/redd/redd_plus_explained/

Ise, J. (1920). *The United States forest policy*. New Haven, CT: Yale University Press.

Linacre, N., Ambrosi, A., & Kossoy, P. (2011). *State and trends of the carbon market 2011*. World Bank, Carbon Finance Unit. Retrieved from http://siteresources.worldbank.org/INTCARBONFINANCE/Resources/StateAndTrend_LowRes.pdf

The Nature Conservancy. (2015). *Bolivia: Noel Kempf Mercado National Park*. Retrieved from http://www.nature.org/ourinitiatives/regions/southamerica/bolivia/placesweprotect/noel-kempff-mercado-park.xml

Nelson, R. H. (1995). *Public lands and private rights: The failure of scientific management*. Lanham, MD: Rowman and Littlefield.

Norway Ministry of Environment and Climate. (2015). *Why NICFI and REDD+?* Retrieved from https://www.regjeringen.no/en/topics/climate-and-environment/climate/climate-and-forest-initiative/kos-innsikt/hvorfor-norsk-regnskogsatsing/id2076569/

Pennsylvania Historical and Museum Commission. (n.d.). *Governor Gifford Pinchot*. Retrieved from http://www.portal.state.pa.us/portal/server.pt/community/1879–1951/4284/gifford_pinchot/469112

The REDD Desk. (2016). *Germany's REDD+ Early Movers Programme*. Retrieved from http://theredddesk.org/markets-standards/germanys-redd-early-movers-programme

Schalatek, L., Nakhooda, S., & Watson, C. (2014). *Climate finance fundamentals: The Green Climate Fund*. Retrieved from http://www.climatefundsupdate.org/resources/finance-fundamentals

Scott, J. C. (1998). *Seeing like a state: How certain schemes to improve the human condition have failed*. New Haven, CT: Yale University Press.

Smith, Z. (2013). *The environmental policy paradox* (6th ed.). Upper Saddle River, NJ: Pearson.

Steen, H. K. (1976). *The U.S. Forest Service: A history*. Seattle: University of Washington Press.

United Nations Collaborative Programme on Reducing Emissions from Deforestation and Forest Degradation in Developing Countries (UN-REDD Programme).

(2008a). *About the UN REDD Programme*. Retrieved from "http://www.un-redd. org/AboutUN-REDDProgramme

United Nations Collaborative Programme on Reducing Emissions from Deforestation and Forest Degradation in Developing Countries (UN-REDD Programme). (2008b). *Framework document*. Retrieved from http://www.un-redd.org/Portals/ 15/documents/publications/UN-REDD_FrameworkDocument.pdf

United Nations Collaborative Programme on Reducing Emissions from Deforestation and Forest Degradation in Developing Countries (UN-REDD Programme). (2011). *The UN-REDD programme strategy: 2011–2015*. Retrieved from http:// www.unredd.net/index.php?view=document&alias=14096-un-redd-pb14-2015- strategic-framework&category_slug=session-3-strategic-and-policy-issues& layout=default&option=com_docman&Itemid=134

United Nations Collaborative Programme on Reducing Emissions from Deforestation and Forest Degradation in Developing Countries (UN-REDD Programme). (2014). *Rules of procedure and operational guidance*. Retrieved from http://www. un-redd.org/AboutUN-REDDProgramme/tabid/102613/Default.aspx

United Nations Framework Convention on Climate Change (UNFCCC). (2007). *Report of the Conference of the Parties on its thirteenth session*. Retrieved from http://unfccc.int/resource/docs/2007/cop13/eng/06a01.pdf

United Nations Framework Convention on Climate Change (UNFCCC). (2011). *Report of the Conference of the Parties on its sixteenth session, held in Cancun from 29 November to 10 December 2010*. Retrieved from http://unfccc.int/ resource/docs/2010/cop16/eng/07a01.pdf#page=2

United Nations Framework Convention on Climate Change (UNFCCC). (2012). *Report of the Conference of the Parties on its seventeenth session, held in Durban from 28 November to 11 December 2011*. Retrieved from http://unfccc.int/ meetings/durban_nov_2011/meeting/6245/php/view/reports.php

United Nations Framework Convention on Climate Change (UNFCCC). (2013). *Report of the Conference of the Parties on its eighteenth session, held in Doha from 26 November to 8 December 2012*. Retrieved from http://unfccc.int/docu mentation/documents/advanced_search/items/6911.php?priref=600007316

United Nations Framework Convention on Climate Change (UNFCCC). (2014a). *Green Climate Fund*. Retrieved from http://unfccc.int/cooperation_and_support/ financial_mechanism/green_climate_fund/items/5869.php

United Nations Framework Convention on Climate Change (UNFCCC). (2014b). *Kyoto Protocol*. Retrieved from http://unfccc.int/kyoto_protocol/items/2830.php

US Environmental Protection Agency. (2009). Endangerment and cause or contribute findings for greenhouse gases under Section 202(a) of the Clean Air Act; final rule. *Federal Register, 74*(239), 66496–66546.

Wiersum, K. F. (1995). 200 years of sustainability in forestry: Lessons from history. *Environmental Management, 18*(3), 321–329.

World Bank. (2015). *History*. Retrieved from http://www.worldbank.org/en/about/ history

World Resources Institute. (2013). *Warsaw Climate Meeting Makes Progress on Forests, REDD+*. Retrieved from http://www.wri.org/blog/2013/12/warsaw-climate- meeting-makes-progress-forests-redd

3 Problems with the definition of a forest and leakage

It is our assertion that carbon credits for forest conservation programs such as Reducing Emissions from Deforestation and Forest Degradation (REDD) as currently constituted will not address the key drivers of deforestation and will accelerate social and environmental problems in the developing world. In this chapter we will provide the facts that lay the basis for that claim. We will also describe why REDD will fail but also argue that the program will benefit only some corporations and governments and leave the planet's balance of carbon unchanged while disrupting the livelihoods of millions of people.

It is much easier and faster to create a desert than to create or maintain a healthy forest. In fact, we are creating deserts by the thousands of hectares each year. Desertification is the process of turning productive land, in this case forests, into wasteland. Desertification is occurring at an alarming pace – particularly in countries in the less developed world. When plants die, through overgrazing, trampling, or harvesting of timber, the moisture retention capacity of the ground is lost and the land is slowly converted to desert.

The loss of forests is driven by many factors including fuel use and production, timber harvesting, clearing of land for animal grazing, and expansion of agriculture. It is widely believed that deforestation accounts for some 20 percent of human-caused greenhouse gas (GHG) emissions. The authors of this book fully understand the problem of deforestation. Unfortunately, we also understand that REDD will not end that problem nor, in the long run, mitigate climate change.

The drivers of deforestation have led to the destruction of natural forests and the rise of tree plantations. REDD will not stop this. Forests will never be saved from degradation and destruction so long as the root cause of deforestation goes unchecked and plantations continue to grow. We will demonstrate below how and why two key international organizations, the United Nations and the World Bank, are unwittingly fostering this destruction in large part by how they define a forest. We will then define leakage and analyze how protection projects are not finding success.

What is a forest?

It has been estimated that there are well over 100 different definitions around the world for what constitutes a forest (Lund, 2007). These definitions take into consideration some combination of various factors including land cover, land use, or declarations by governments and administrative units (Lund, 2007). There are other ways that forests can be further categorized based on any combination of diversity of species, management characteristics (whether natural or planted for harvesting wood), amount of precipitation, crown cover, and average height of trees. As you can see, what seems like a simple task – creating a universally accepted definition of a forest – quickly becomes rather complex and difficult.

Why is it important to have a consistent definition of what is considered to be a forest? Research shows that the definition of a forest is important for measuring real emissions reductions and the land that can be considered as a potential REDD project. The definition of a forest determines deforestation and forest degradation rates as well as identifying the drivers of deforestation (Romijn et al., 2015). For example, if one country considers a forest to have a minimum of 20 percent crown cover per hectare while another considers land with only 10 percent crown cover to be forest, and both have enrolled the same number of hectares in REDD, then the country with 20 percent crown cover is capturing more carbon. This is not a problem since they would be compensated based on the amount of carbon captured. Differences in definitions between countries are problematic, however, when determining the extent of leakage internationally and measuring whether global emissions reductions are being achieved. However, the definition of a forest becomes a problem within a country when one seeks to determine the drivers of deforestation and measure future deforestation and forest degradation. It impacts the estimated magnitude of deforestation and forest degradation (Romijn et al., 2015). It is also important to distinguish between a natural forest and a tree plantation. If the two are not distinguished, a natural forest could be cut down and replaced with a plantation and this may not be captured as being deforestation. Without an accurate international measurement of deforestation and forest degradation, it is almost impossible to determine how much leakage is occurring and whether or not GHG emissions are being reduced on a global scale.

Forests are loosely defined under the United Nations Collaborative Programme on Reducing Emissions from Deforestation and Forest Degradation in Developing Countries (UN-REDD Programme) and the World

Bank's Forest Carbon Partnership Facility. The United Nations Framework Convention on Climate Change (UNFCCC) provides a range for height and canopy cover to delineate a forest. There must be 10–30 percent crown cover with the trees reaching 2–5 meters (Romijn et al., 2015). The UNFCCC's definition does not consider land use. Conversely, the definition of the Food and Agriculture Organization (FAO) does consider land use. Land used predominantly for agriculture cannot be considered a forest. A forest is defined by the FAO (2000) as land spanning more than 0.5 hectares with more than 10 percent tree canopy cover and trees higher than 5 meters (or having the potential to reach a height of 5 meters). The World Bank has two definitions of a forest. One definition has a forest area as "land under natural or planted stands of trees of at least 5 meters in situ, whether productive or not" (World Bank, 2012). Another definition is the World Bank's operating policy (2002), which states that the area must have a minimum tree crown cover of 10 percent and the trees must have the potential to reach a minimum height of 2 meters.

Types of forests

The United Nations has chosen to define forests in a way that includes primary forests, secondary forests, and plantations. The term primary forest describes forests that fit the typical image most people have: an area of natural growth with no obvious indications of human involvement. These are areas filled with native flora and fauna that have had no previous large disturbances. Fewer and fewer of these forests exist today. Primary forests are "generally more resilient (and stable, resistant, and adaptive)" (Secretariat of the Convention on Biological Diversity, 2010, p. 2). Secondary forests are also covered in the UNFCCC definition. These are areas that are expected to revert to natural forests. Unlike primary forests, secondary forests have been impacted by disturbances, both human and natural, such as logging, mining, landslides, agriculture, and fire. These areas can regenerate naturally or artificially when such measures as replanting are taken. These two types of land, primary and secondary, are generally accepted as forests. However, calling a plantation a forest strikes us bordering on disingenuous.

A plantation is an area of land that is cultivated for commercial purposes. These areas are normally composed of a single type of vegetation (a monoculture). Many plantations use genetically altered trees. Genetic altering of trees is done by scientists to breed "supertrees" that are fast growing. Scientists choose the fastest growing, most pest- and disease-resistant stands in an area, and from each stand, the very best tree is chosen. It is called a "plus" tree, and the top is taken off to use for grafts, which are placed on sprouting tree roots of the same species. The roots "read" the graft, and the tree grows to be an exact replica of the "plus" tree. Thus, a genetically engineered tree is born. The tree is grown in a container until it is large enough to plant out in a tree plantation. Even though the trees are developed from the best quality of trees, they still require intensive amounts of herbicides and pesticides because they are planted as a monocrop. Their lack of genetic diversity makes them susceptible to disease and pests. Genetic engineering also limits the available gene pool for new trees to grow in a particular area.

Many of the countries that participate in REDD and other forest-based programs have agricultural plantations. There are, for example, teak and eucalyptus plantations in India, palm oil plantations in the Congo Basin and Indonesia, and rubber tree plantations in Thailand. As stated by Gupta, Van der Grijp, and Kuik, "large industrial tree plantations dominate in subtropical and temperate South America. South and East Asia contain the largest share of the world's tree plantations . . ." (2013, p. 27).

Tree plantations are becoming more common around the globe. In 2010 the FAO reported that 264 million hectares of forest were some type of plantations, amounting to approximately 6.6 percent of the world's forests (FAO, 2010, p. 90). Plantations create serious problems that lead to the continued destruction of forests.

What's wrong with plantations?

Monoculture plantations severely inhibit, if not end, the ability of forests to naturally maintain their ecosystem balance or resilience and severely limit the biodiversity of the forest ecosystem. Ecosystem resilience, the capacity of an ecosystem to bounce back from disruptions like fire, is fundamentally important for the health and longevity of an ecosystem. In a natural forest, an ecosystem is established based on the interaction of a variety of plants, animals, fungi, insects, and other organisms. Each species is part of the forest's natural ecosystem interdependence. When natural disturbances such as fires and floods arrive, resilient ecosystems are able to rebuild themselves. However, plantations limit these interactions by destroying the natural habitats, food sources, and life in the area. Managers of mono-agricultural systems, like monoculture forests, have an incentive to drive out competing species or any organism that might interfere with the growth of the agricultural product. This is accomplished by the use of pesticides and herbicides, among other means. When planting forests becomes a business, monoculture forestry thrives, and resilience and biodiversity are decreased, to the detriment of the larger ecosystem of which the plantation is a part. The people who depended on those once-forested lands are displaced, and their social and cultural worlds disturbed. Perhaps there is little we can do about this in many developing countries, but is it not something the West and the more developed world should subsidize.

One example of this sad reality is in Kalimantan (the Indonesian portion of Borneo), where millions of hectares of land have been converted into plantations (discussed in more detail in later chapters). In this vast expanse of land, 46 endangered mammal species were identified (Venter et al., 2009, p. 125). Even small changes in biodiversity in the Indonesian forest can have overwhelming impacts on these endangered species (Lang, 2012).

It should also be noted that in addition to the biodiversity and resilience problems noted above, plantations also consume significant amounts of energy, fertilizer, and fossil fuels. Hence, the environmental degradation occurring on the ground is not only the result of the monoculture agriculture but also of all the negative environmental spinoffs associated with that monoculture. While plantations may look like forests because they provide a green cover to the land, they are in fact dangerous and harmful to the landscape and the people. Plantations have been called "green deserts" in Brazil, a "green cancer" in South Africa, and "green soldiers" in Chile (Langelle et al., 2006). They rob the land of biodiversity and are planted in rows like marching soldiers – locals know what plantations bring.

The undesirability of plantations comes into play when we understand the role of selling carbon credits. REDD credits may be available for a newly planted forest if it is established that the area being planted is not already a forest and is in fact degraded land – this is what we refer to as afforestation. Such a trade-off could lead to reductions in carbon being emitted into the atmosphere. But it still leaves the negative impacts on local populations, leakage, and the resilience and biodiversity problems.

As of 2016, REDD funds are not being used to protect plantations developed in areas that were previously primary or secondary forests. But as we have seen, the definition of forest that is being used does not preclude this from happening in the future. At current rates of compensation it is clear that monoculture agriculture, at least in the case of palm oil, is more profitable than conserving forests in exchange for REDD compensation (Koh & Butler, 2007). So land continues to be converted to palm oil and other plantations in spite of REDD. Can the day be far off when the maturity of these plantations reaches a point where it is advantageous for the owners to retire the trees and seek REDD funds rather than tear down the trees and replant? At that point will the plantation owners simply move on to more primary or secondary forest and plant new plantations?

This scenario has a disturbing similarity to the California Land Conservation Act (California Code, 2015), also known as the Williamson Act. That legislation provided agricultural landowners with property tax relief in return for not converting their land for a higher economic use. Agricultural land in California, as in most of the United States, is taxed on its highest and best economic use. The highest use is usually for a development, such as a housing subdivision or shopping mall. This means that land that is in agriculture is taxed at the value of that land for some other higher-value use, such as a subdivision of new homes. The problem was that the Williamson Act merely delayed property taxes until some later date when the property was sold – land speculators could buy farms and keep farming until the market price for land increased, and then they would sell. This is in fact what happened in many parts of California. At the time of the sale a property owner could reap the full value of the property. Consequently, the Williamson Act preserved agricultural property for a while at great cost to local governments that were dependent on that property tax. Eventually the land, as anyone who is been to Southern California can attest, became subdivisions and shopping centers anyway.

REDD has the potential to act as a kind of Williamson Act in reverse. Landowners can convert primary and secondary forest into plantations today. They reap the benefits of agricultural production for the life of the trees in the plantation. And then, we suspect, REDD comes in to prevent the destruction of those plantations. Nothing, of course, keeps the plantation corporations from then moving on to another area and creating a new plantation – what we might call plantation leakage. Obviously, this is speculation on our part. But given the way REDD has been set up, it is not implausible that this is how it will play out.

Inefficient carbon sequestration

As stated by Mutter and Overbeek (2011), "monoculture oil palm, eucalyptus, rubber, and jatropha plantations are expanding . . . Locating such plantations in the South allows polluting projects in the North to continue business as usual, due to the idea of the carbon tradeoff." If the goal is to sequester carbon, then tree plantations are not practical carbon sequestration projects. The cost of clearing the land for the development of plantations and the slow rate at which the carbon is sequestered point to the absurdity of the claim that plantations are efficient carbon sequesters. First, land clearing releases more carbon than is absorbed. In Indonesia many biologically diverse peatlands are being destroyed and replaced with oil palm plantations. A study published by the US National Academy of Sciences found that not only were the plantations destroying biodiversity, but the clearance and replacement of peatlands contributed to a higher amount of carbon emissions (Lian Pin et al., 2011, p. 5131). Clearly, the clearing of land for plantations contributes to more carbon emissions, making plantations impractical sequesters.

Next, carbon is absorbed slowly in plantations. A study done on various tree species in Australia calculated the average plantation size needed to offset 1000 metric tons of carbon emissions within 30 years. It found that it took from 1 hectare of eucalyptus to 45 hectares of hoop pine to offset 1000 metric tons of carbon emissions (Grace & Basso, 2012). The US Environmental Protection Agency estimates that 1000 metric tons of carbon is similar to the carbon footprint of 138 homes or 212 passenger vehicles in one year. Waiting 30 years to make up for a very small amount of carbon emissions seems impractical. It is clear that given the clearing of land for plantations and the slow rate at which carbon is absorbed, plantations cannot survive under the carbon sequestering claim. This is particularly true when there are so many ways to sequester carbon (Surampalli et al., 2015).

As we have noted, there are severe limitations on the use of plantations to secure REDD funding. We have also noted that plantations play a role in REDD and have the potential to play a much greater role in the future. Nonetheless, we feel that leakage problems are the primary reason the REDD will fail.

Leakage: is it all for nothing?

Many forest conservation programs, including REDD, encounter leakage problems. Leakage is the unanticipated increase in emissions outside a protected area. There are several types of leakage – REDD will lead to them all and hence prove incapable of reducing carbon overall. The simplest and most direct leakage occurs when a forest conservation measure displaces indigenous peoples. A plot of land that becomes protected may drive farmers to clear another area. One area is protected, but an adjacent or nearby area, previously undeveloped, is destroyed. There is also market leakage and activity-shifting leakage.

Market leakage

Market leakage simply refers to changes in market conditions that can shift an activity from one place to another. For example, if the supply of timber in one region diminishes, we can expect markets to act to make up the shortfall in other areas – putting pressure on other forests and leading to deforestation in another area. This is the simple operation of supply and demand. The net gain to the environment is therefore eliminated.

A study of forestry in China illustrates the point. When the Chinese government implemented a national logging quota in order to preserve its forests, researchers Hu, Shi, and Hodges (2014) examined the quotas implemented by the government and predicted that restrictions on logging would have a profound effect on global timber prices. Such restrictions would inevitably lead to increased timber production in other parts of the world.

Activity-shifting leakage

Forest protection projects and plantations also cause activity-shifting leakage. Activity-shifting leakage refers to the movement of carbon-emitting projects to a new location when REDD or another conservation project has closed off an area. Yasuni National Park in Ecuador provides a good example of this type of leakage. Known for its biodiversity and home to two uncontacted indigenous groups, the park drew international attention when President Rafael Correa announced plans to drill for oil in the park. He offered to call off the drilling projects if international organizations would compensate Ecuador US$3.6 billion. Although this offer would mitigate an estimated 410 million tons of carbon emissions and protect biodiversity and human rights, many argued that protecting the Yasuni National Park would only cause oil drilling to be moved to another part of Ecuador. In the end, the international community did not collect enough money to meet the president's demand and the oil drilling project commenced (Watts, 2013). The international community saw that the oil, for which demand is largely inelastic, would be extracted either within the park or outside of the park. This example demonstrates the risk for activity-shifting leakage but also illustrates the transformation of forests into economic commodities.

Another example of activity-shifting leakage occurred in southern Chile. With the spread of eucalyptus plantations, the indigenous Mapuche population saw the devastation of their traditional lands and lives. In the Lumaco region of Chile, plantations have spread from 14 percent of the land in 1988 to 52 percent of the land in 2002. Today 2,400,000 hectares are covered by monoculture eucalyptus plantations (Carruthers & Rodriguez, 2009; Gerber, 2011). This expansion has caused Mapuche populations to become dependent on water trucks instead of the traditional natural water sources; in addition, pesticides and pollen have increased the yearly number of illnesses within the community. Many Mapuche have chosen to move to cities in order to avoid further impoverishment now that their traditional lifestyle is under attack. Again, in both these examples of activity-shifting leakage in Ecuador and Chile, the demand on the land did not diminish. REDD projects induce leakage; instead of reducing deforestation and carbon emissions, they only shift these somewhere else.

Unfortunately, there is no realistic way to address leakage. Global demand for wood fiber will create markets wherever that fiber can be produced. To the extent that leakage is caused by the demand for timber for building,

alternatives are available. These materials include plastics made from recy-
clables, hemp, and other fibers that can be grown sustainably and faster than
wood. However, we should not expect subsistence farmers and those gathering wood for fuel to find alternatives unless they are provided.

Temporal leakage

Temporal leakage deals with time and the permanence of the conservation
project. If a forest is conserved for 40 years and then is deforested, those
GHG gases are emitted into the air, regardless of the conservation project; it
just happened at a later date. In this example of temporal leakage, the GHG
gases were released after 40 years. Temporal leakage can be extremely
destructive because it results in a rather quick release of large amounts of
stored carbon. Temporal leakage would negate past climate change mitigation efforts.

Leakage and ecosystem resilience

Avoided deforestation can decrease ecosystem resilience. Furthermore,
attempting to implement REDD universally, which is the main way to avoid
leakage and actually achieve a net decrease in carbon, can collapse ecosystems. To understand the relationship of REDD to long-term forest health,
a little ecology is in order. The adaptive cycle best explains the concept
of ecosystem resilience. There are four stages of the cycle: (1) growth or
exploitation, (2) conservation, (3) collapse or release, and (4) reorganization. The phase of shifting between stages 1 and 2 is characterized by incre-
mental growth and accumulation. The phase shifting between stages 3 and
4 is caused by an external disturbance that leads to rapid reorganization and
eventually renewal. Any policy that will mitigate climate change while preserving forests must allow the adaptive cycle to run its course.

REDD as currently constituted is contrary to the adaptive cycle and the
preservation of ecosystem resilience. Unless REDD is used to protect primary forests and biodiversity, it will deplete ecosystem resilience. REDD,
as it currently stands, will do just that because it allows for monoculture tree
plantations to be considered as forests.

The transition from exploitation of natural resources to conservation and
then to release is a slow-moving process. However, the change from release
to reorganization of the ecosystem is rapid and can result in a qualitative
change to the ecosystem. To better understand how this cycle works, let's
use a primary forest as an example. As a primary forest grows, biodiversity
increases. Various organisms have a niche within this emerging ecosystem,
and they become interconnected as the forest continues to grow. At the end

of the growth stage, this interconnectedness leads the ecosystem to self-regulate through a high level of efficiency, meaning that redundancies such as nitrogen fixing are phased out. When a disturbance to the ecosystem takes place, like a forest fire or an outbreak of pests, the system cannot adjust to the sudden disturbance and collapses. REDD, if used to protect primary forests, could maintain this resiliency.

While the above example illustrates natural environmental processes and disturbances, the collapse of ecosystems and their inability to regenerate are magnified by human actions. If the "forest" is a tree plantation, rather than a primary forest, the depletion of resilience is magnified. A tree plantation that consists of genetically engineered trees that grow more rapidly than the original species of the tree lacks biodiversity, making it less able to adapt to disturbances. In some cases, REDD will allow for tree plantations to be considered forests, thus depleting the resiliency of ecosystems. Tree plantations are more susceptible to disturbances and as a result are more susceptible to collapse and the release of stored carbon.

This is an explanation of just a single forest. When taking a larger scale into consideration, such as multiple forests within a country or in many countries, the harm can be much more significant. Avoided deforestation, done in an attempt to store carbon, makes a forest more likely to collapse at a much faster rate. This inevitably causes more carbon to be released.

Additionality

One further, often troubling concept need to be covered here – additionality. Additionality is the extremely difficult determination of what carbon reductions might have happened in the absence of the REDD project. This is important because an offset needs to represent a real reduction in GHG emissions. If the amount of carbon released is no different either with or without the project, then purchased offsets are not offsetting anything. As one might imagine, determining whether projected reductions in emissions are additional to what would have happened if the project was not built is difficult at best.

REDD should not pay for protection of a forest that would otherwise be protected. One way to avoid additionality problems would be to target those areas for REDD protection that are most likely to be deforested. These might those adjacent to land that had recently been deforested. As Harris noted (2014, p. 502), "there is the risk that targeting high risk forests could create perverse incentives. Governments or forest owners could announce they intended to convert forests to alternative uses. Speculators could buy high value forests then threaten to fell them unless they were compensated."

Winners and losers?

Critics of REDD often argue that the program has led to the commodification of forests. In a sense that is true, but we don't find that a compelling criticism. Globalization has led to the commodification of natural resources all over the planet. What REDD has done is facilitate this commodification by creating a market, for carbon offsets, that did not exist before. From an environmental perspective this may prevent some carbon from entering the atmosphere (highly unlikely in our opinion because of leakage problems), but it does nothing to decrease the overall amount of carbon currently in the atmosphere. Stated another way, it gives a free pass to corporations in the more developed world to continue polluting. "The biggest buyers of REDD credits are the worst polluters – big oil and big coal," says Bill Barclay, the Rainforest Action Network's research director. "They are looking for a cheap 'get out of jail free card' – it's basically green-washing" (quoted in Arsenault, 2010).

More than 1.6 billion people are connected to forests in some way for their livelihoods. But only a small percentage of these people own the forests they are dependent on (Bele, Sonwa, & Tiani, 2015). This is the main reason that leakage is such a problem. Decisions about forest practices are made by people not directly impacted by the forest. Indigenous peoples, farmers, or others who need the forest to survive, collect firewood, or gather or hunt for food will seek out alternatives when governments or people from the outside decide how their forest should be used.

Finally, it should be noted that the countries that suffer from the most serious deforestation are also the countries that historically are likely to have governance problems – notably corruption, often in the form of logging (Bofin et al., 2011). It has been noted that "forest management in the developing world has long been fraught with corruption" (Brown, 2010, p. 237) and, furthermore, that "anti-corruption policies limited to the forest sector are unlikely to work in countries with high corruption levels, which require systemic institutional changes" (Tacconi, Downs, & Larmour, 2009, p. 167). Although many countries, like Indonesia, have taken steps to prevent corruption, it remains a serious risk (Dermawan & Sinaga, 2015).

In the last chapter we will discuss in greater detail our suggestions for improving REDD. Here we would like to point out that both the funding for REDD and the distribution of the funds are key factors that limit its success. There must be enough money under the current REDD regime to entice landowners and controllers to save the forest and forgo development. In addition, issues with monitoring are tied closely to the future economic failure of REDD. Efficient monitoring systems are expensive and time consuming. The implementation of Measurement, Reporting, and Verification systems in participating countries is currently the largest financial drain on REDD. These systems oversee the effects of curbing deforestation and are supposed to help REDD in its transparency promise.

In the next chapter we will discuss the implementation of REDD and describe how some of the problems discussed above have already begun to manifest themselves.

References

Arsenault, C. (2010, Dec. 10). Seeing REDD on climate change. *Al Jazeera*. Retrieved from http://www.aljazeera.com/indepth/features/2010/12/201012919238402389.html

Bele, M. Y., Sonwa, D. J., & Tiani, A. M. (2015). Adapting the Congo Basin forests management to climate change: Linkages among biodiversity, forest loss, and human well-being. *Forest Policy and Economics, 50*, 1–10.

Bofin, P., du Preez, M. L., Standing, A., & Williams, A. (2011). *REDD integrity: Addressing governance and corruption challenges in schemes for reducing emissions from deforestation and forest degradation (REDD)*. U4 Report, 1. Bergin, Norway: Chr. Michelsen Institute.

Brown, M. L. (2010). Limiting corrupt incentives in a global REDD regime. *Ecology LQ, 37*, 237–268.

California Code. (2015). Chapter 7. Article 1, Section 51200.

Carruthers, D., & Rodriguez, P. (2009). Mapuche protest, environmental conflict and social movement linkage in Chile. *Third World Quarterly, 30*(4), 743–760.

Dermawan, A., & Sinaga, A. C. (2015). *Towards REDD+ integrity: Opportunities and challenges for Indonesia*. U4 Issue, 5. Bergin, Norway: Chr. Michelsen Institute.

Food and Agriculture Organization (FAO). (2000). *On definitions of forest and forest change*. Forest Resources Assessment Programme. Working Paper No. 33. Rome, Italy.

Food and Agriculture Organization (FAO). (2010). *Global forest resources assessment 2010: Main report*. FAO Forestry Paper 163. Retrieved from http://www.fao.org/docrep/013/i1757e/i1757e.pdf

Gerber, J. F. (2011). Conflicts over industrial tree plantations in the South: Who, how and why? *Global Environmental Change, 21*(1), 165–176.

Grace, P. R., & Basso, B. (2012). Offsetting greenhouse gas emissions through biological carbon sequestration in North Eastern Australia. *Agricultural Systems, 105*(1), 1–6. http://dx.doi.org/10.1016/j.agsy.2011.08.006

Gupta, J., Van der Grijp, N., & Kuik, O. (2013). *Climate change, forests and REDD: lessons for institutional design*. New York, NY: Routledge.

Harris, P. G. (2014). *Routledge handbook of global environmental politics*. New York, NY: Routledge.

Hu, X., Shi, G., & Hodges, D. (2014). International market leakage from China's forest policies. *Forests, 5*(11), 2613–2625. http://dx.doi.org/10.3390/f5112613

Koh, L. P., & Butler, R. A. (2007). Can REDD make natural forests competitive with oil palm? *ITTO Tropical Forest Update, 19*(1), 9.

Lang, C. (2012, Oct.). Oil palm plantations replacing forests in Kalimantan. *REDD Monitor*. Retrieved from http://www.redd-monitor.org/2012/10/10/oil-palm-plantations-replacing-forests-in-kalimantan/

Langelle, O., Petermann, A., Perry, A., Carman, N., & Tokar, B. (2006). Ecological and social impacts of fast growing timber plantations and genetically engineered trees. Paper presented at the International Union of Forestry Research Organizations Forest Plantations Meeting: Sustainable Forest Management with Fast Growing Plantations, Charleston, SC, October.

Lian Pin, K., Miettinen, J., Soo Chin, L., & Gazoul, J. (2011). Remotely sensed evidence of tropical peatland conversion to oil palm. *Proceedings of the National Academy of Sciences of the United States of America, 108*(12), 5127–5132. http://dx.doi.org/10.1073/pnas.1018776108

Lund, H. G. (coord.). (2007). *Definitions of forest, deforestation, afforestation, and reforestation.* Gainesville, VA: Forest Information Services. Retrieved from http://home.comcast.net/_gyde/DEFpaper.htm

Mutter, R. N., & Overbeek, W. (2011, Oct. 20). *The great lie: Monoculture trees as forests.* United Nations Research Institute for Social Development. Retrieved from http://www.unrisd.org/80256B3C005BE6B5/search/531DAFFB8B319F69C125792E00499ED1?OpenDocument

Romijn, E., Lantican, C. B., Herold, M., Lindquist, E., Ochieng, R., Wijaya, A., ... & Verchot, L. (2015). Assessing change in national forest monitoring capacities of 99 tropical countries. *Forest Ecology and Management, 352*, 109–123.

Secretariat of the Convention on Biological Diversity. (2010). *Biodiversity is essential for investments in forests and carbon.* Retrieved from https://www.cbd.int/forest/doc/ts41/ts41mainmsgs-en.pdf

Surampalli, R. Y., Zhang, T. C., Tyagi, R. D., Naidu, R., Gurjar, B. R., Ojha, C. S. P., ... & Kao, C. M. (2015). *Carbon capture and storage: Physical, chemical, and biological methods.* Reston, VA: American Society of Civil Engineers.

Tacconi, L., Downs, F., & Larmour, P. (2009). Anti-corruption policies in the forest sector and REDD+. In A. Angelsen & M. Brockhaus (Eds.), *Realising REDD+: National strategy and policy options*, 163–174. Barat, Indonesia: Center for International Forestry Research (CIFOR).

United Nations Environment Programme. (n.d.). *Forest definition and extent.* Retrieved from http://www.unep.org/vitalforest/Report/VFG-01-Forest-definition-and-extent.pdf

Venter, O., Meijaard, E., Possingham, H., Dennis, R., Sheil, D., Wich, S., & Wilson, K. (2009). Carbon payments as a safeguard for threatened tropical mammals. *Conservation Letters, 2*(3), 123–129. http://dx.doi.org/10.1111/j.1755-263X.2009.00059.x

Watts, J. (2013, Aug. 16). Ecuador approves Yasuni National Park oil drilling in Amazon rainforest. *The Guardian.* Retrieved from http://www.theguardian.com/world/2013/aug/16/ecuador-approves-yasuni-amazon-oil-drilling

World Bank. (2002). *Operating policy 4.36*. Retrieved from http://web.worldbank. org/WBSITE/EXTERNAL/PROJECTS/EXTPOLICIES/EXTOPMANUAL/0,, contentMDK:20066710~menuPK:64701637~pagePK:64709096~piPK:64709108~theSitePK:502184,00.html

World Bank. (2012). *Agricultural and rural development*. Retrieved from http:// data.worldbank.org/about/world-development-indicators-data/agriculture-and-rural-development

4 REDD partner countries and drivers of deforestation

Introduction

The first project in the style of Reducing Emissions from Deforestation and Forest Degradation (REDD) was the Noel Kempff Mercado Climate Action Project, conceived in 1997 and located in northeastern Bolivia. It was a joint partnership project between the government of Bolivia, the Fundación Amigos de la Naturaleza (Friends of Nature Foundation, a non-profit conservation organization headquartered in Santa Cruz, Bolivia), the Nature Conservancy (the world's largest conservation organization, headquartered in Arlington, Virginia), American Electric Power (an electric utility company headquartered in Columbus, Ohio), BP Amoco (a major petroleum company headquartered in London), and PacifiCorp (an electric utility company headquartered in Portland, Oregon). This project was an integral part of Clean Development Mechanism standards for afforestation and reforestation to protect approximately four million acres of threatened tropical forests in the Department of Santa Cruz, Bolivia, for at least 30 years.

Currently, according to the United Nations, the United Nations Collaborative Programme on Reducing Emissions from Deforestation and Forest Degradation in Developing Countries (UN-REDD Programme) supports 60 partner countries across Africa, Asia-Pacific, and Latin America and the Caribbean. To date, the REDD Policy Board has approved a total of US$67.8 million for national programs in 21 partner countries. These funds support the development and implementation of National REDD Plus Strategies. The REDD program regional teams operate in all three areas noted above to help coordinate efforts across countries in each region and liaise with other regional teams to ensure all countries can benefit from knowledge sharing and learn important lessons from one another. In Asia-Pacific, the program currently supports 16 partner countries. Nine countries, namely, Bangladesh, Cambodia, Indonesia, Mongolia, Papua New Guinea, the Philippines, the Solomon Islands, Sri Lanka, and Vietnam, receive direct support for their National UN-REDD Program. Other REDD program partner countries in Asia-Pacific include Bhutan, Lao People's Democratic Republic, Malaysia, Myanmar, Nepal, and Pakistan. In Africa the program is working with 24 countries: Benin, Burkina Faso, Cameroon, the Central African Republic, Chad, Congo, Cote d'lvoire, the Democratic Republic of the Congo, Equatorial Guinea, Ethiopia, Gabon, Ghana, Guinea Bissau, Madagascar, Malawi, Morocco, Nigeria, South Sudan, Sudan, Tanzania, Tunisia, Uganda, Zambia, and Zimbabwe. The 16 REDD partner countries in Latin America and the Caribbean include Argentina, Bolivia, Chile, Colombia, Costa Rica, the Dominican Republic, Ecuador, El Salvador, Guatemala, Guyana, Honduras, Mexico, Panama, Paraguay, Peru, and Suriname. These countries benefit from receiving targeted support from the UN-REDD Programme for national actions. They also engage with the program in a number of ways, including as observers to the program's Policy Board, and through participation in regional workshops and unique knowledge-sharing opportunities. In the next section, we turn to 12 case studies to identify drivers of deforestation in the different countries and regions.

Drivers of deforestation

International institutions are negotiating various strategies and policies to mitigate greenhouse gas (GHG) emissions from forests. REDD and/or REDD Plus are the strategies being practiced for reducing deforestation. It is believed that the strategies used to reduce deforestation not only help mitigate emissions but also sustain livelihoods for rural poor and indigenous people and preserve biological diversity. Market approaches are evolving to provide monetary compensation for preserving the forests. Although strategies and policies directed at reducing deforestation are central to decreasing emissions, many challenges remain to be addressed for implementing REDD and REDD Plus programs. Yet the benefits from these programs are not easily achieved as they come with a bundle of challenges related to implementing them locally and achieving the goal of reducing GHGs globally. There are various direct and indirect/underlying causes of deforestation and forest degradation. Since the 1980s several attempts have been made to explain the causes of tropical deforestation (A. S. Mather & Needle, 2000). Clearly, drivers and causes of deforestation may not be reduced to a few variables. Understanding the underlying and apparent causes of deforestation provides deep insights for formulating and implementing effective policies to address the complex drivers of deforestation and forest degradation.

Although the drivers of deforestation differ from country to country, region to region, and continent to continent, they can still be narrowed down and discussed to understand their implications for the success or failure of the REDD strategies and future policy guidelines. The causes of deforestation can be classified as direct and indirect/underlying, or internal and external, drivers of deforestation and forest degradation. In general, the direct/internal causes of deforestation include land-use change for large-scale or small-scale agriculture (Meyer & Turner, 1992). Deforestation for large-scale agriculture is mainly driven by improved agricultural technology for production of soybeans, palm oil, biofuels, and meat. Increasing populations, soil infertility, and subsistence agricultural expansion are indirect drivers, which usually drive deforestation for small-scale agriculture. Other important drivers of deforestation are mineral extraction, fuelwood consumption, road development, infrastructure development, commercial logging, weak land tenure, and corrupt governance. The interplay of several of these direct and underlying drivers has been driving deforestation in a synergistically robust way. Now we discuss the regional and national drivers of deforestation by doing representative studies of a total of 12 countries from Asia-Pacific, Africa, and Latin America and the Caribbean.

Drivers of deforestation in the Asia-Pacific region

The Asia-Pacific region has already lost much of its natural forestlands, while the demand for paper, agricultural products, timber, and meat is driving the destruction of the world's last ancient forests in Indonesia, the Amazon, and the Congo (Greenpeace, n.d.). Scientists and conservationists working in Asia-Pacific nations say the region now stands at a crossroads because of its accelerating rate of deforestation (Drollette, 2013). The "rapid development in Vietnam and the surrounding nations of the greater Mekong region is on the way to accomplishing what American defoliation missions could not: The widespread destruction of Indochina's forests and the biodiversity they harbor" (Drollette, 2013). Although some large blocks of forest remain intact, the pace of deforestation is dizzying, threatening the region's remarkable biodiversity. Illegal logging, subsistence farming, intensive agriculture and cattle ranching, plantations and dams, and unchecked economic development are taking a devastating toll on the forests in the Asia (Butler, 2012a; Drollette, 2013).

Planned and unplanned conversions of forests for agriculture are significant drivers of deforestation in Vietnam. Much of this is due to the high price of rubber and the valuable source of food that cassava provides. Cash crops such as coffee, tea, and pepper as well as shrimp farms are responsible for a proportion of planned conversions. Planned conversion to forest plantations is also a significant driver of deforestation. This is actually a result of recent forest policy that made cheap credit available for those entering plantation forestry. Typhoons have also caused a great amount of deforestation, and their impacts are greater in areas of reduced deforestation.

New infrastructure and hydropower have resulted in deforestation in recent years. Much of the forest degradation that occurs in Vietnam is a result of legal and illegal logging done in an unsustainable fashion. As a result of this driver, the government has placed a ban on logging in natural production forests unless the forest has received sustainable forest management certification (Ministry of Agriculture and Rural Development, Vietnam, 2014).

Cambodia has many direct and indirect drivers of deforestation and forest degradation. Limited capacity and funds to implement sustainable forest management, illegal timber harvesting, forestland clearance, rural poverty, population growth, lack of financial incentives for forest conservation, regional dynamics, and forest fires have been identified as the major drivers of deforestation in Cambodia (Royal Government of Cambodia, 2008). Rapid increases in industrial agricultural expansion with the production of rubber, sugarcane, and biofuels, as well as foreign direct investment in their production, have also been closely linked to deforestation and human rights abuses (UN-REDD Programme, 2011). Economic Land Concessions (ELCs) – a type of legal contract and a subcategory of conversion forests – primarily center on economic gain instead of conservation of the forest. The state distributes ELCs to private or public entities to promote large-scale agricultural developments, plantations, and the oil and mining industries. ELCs are regulated by two legal documents: the Land Law (2001) and the Sub-Decree on Economic Land Concessions (2005). The Land Law states that ELCs can be granted for a period of 99 years and can only be allocated to areas of the state's private land, which excludes "natural origin" forests, which should be classified as public state land. However, several concessions have been made in forested areas and within protected areas, and in some cases the maximum threshold number of hectares allowed (i.e., 10,000 hectares) has been exceeded (R. Mather, 2012). Not surprisingly indirect drivers of deforestation are also linked to the imports and exports of Cambodia. Top exports include clothing, timber, rubber, rice, fish, tobacco, and footwear to the United States, Canada, Germany, the United Kingdom, and Vietnam, and the top imports include petroleum products, cigarettes, construction materials, machinery, raw materials, and pharmaceutical products from Thailand, Vietnam, China, and Singapore (Economy Watch, 2010b).

Indonesia has lost at least 15.79 million hectares of forestland in the last century and has become the most deforested country in the world. There are many causes of deforestation in Indonesia, which include use of forests for fuel, housing and urbanization, commercial logging for items such as paper and furniture, palm oil, biofuels, and cattle ranching. Common methods of deforestation are burning trees and clear cutting. These tactics leave the land completely barren and are controversial practices. Planned deforestation generally represents government-planned changes in forest-area function in the interests of estate crop, agriculture, or housing develop-ments, conducted legitimately in accordance with the law. Ministry of For-estry data show that the area of forestland converted for agriculture and estate crops has continued to increase. The area covered by government decrees regarding forest release reached about 4.5 million hectares in 2002, increasing to 4.7 million hectares in 2007 and then to 4.9 million hectares in 2010 (Indrarto et al., 2012). Note that 70 percent of Indonesia's land area is categorized as forest area (*kawasan hutan*), of which 12 percent is set aside for future conversion. This indicates that some of the deforestation occur-ring in Indonesia was planned for the purposes of development. Unplanned deforestation refers to deforestation resulting from illegal activities such as illegal harvesting, and timber theft has also been ongoing. Degradation due to illegal logging leaves areas vulnerable to further deforestation, because degraded forest is easier to clear. In addition, forest fires and land fires con-stitute another cause of deforestation in Indonesia.

The island of New Guinea has one of the last great expanses of tropi-cal rainforest. Although much of this area is still untouched and in some remote regions natives may have never seen a white-skinned person, the rainforest is rapidly being developed in more accessible regions. Intensive agricultural expansion, commercial logging, and mining are three major causes of deforestation and forest degradation in Papua New Guinea. Each year 50,000–60,000 hectares are cleared totally and permanently: 50 per-cent for agriculture, 25–30 percent for industrial logging, and the rest for infrastructure (Butler, 2006b). However, up to 100,000 additional hectares are affected by selective logging, and almost all logging in New Guinea is conducted by Malaysian logging firms. The country's high population growth rate means increasing amounts of land are converted for subsis-tence agriculture. Typically fire is used for land clearing, and at times – especially during dry El Niño years – agricultural fires can burn out of control. The Papuan government has been slow to address mining pollution and associated deforestation because of the importance of mining for the national economy. Papua New Guinea's rich mineral endowments, coupled with petroleum, account for 25 percent of the gross domestic product and 72 percent of export revenue (Butler, 2006b).

Drivers of deforestation in Latin America and the Caribbean

Anthropogenic drivers of deforestation and forest degradation in Latin America and the Caribbean are mainly centered on large-scale agricultural expansion, small-scale agricultural expansion, and cattle ranching (Bel-lassen et al., 2008). The tropical forests of Latin America are the largest in the world, stretching from southern Brazil to Mexico and Bolivia. It is estimated that an average of 1.8 million hectares of Amazon rainforest was lost annually between 1988 and 2008 – about a third of global tropical deforestation (Foley et al., 2007). In the 1990s high global beef prices are said to have increased deforestation significantly. More recently soybean, sugarcane, and biofuel crop production and cattle ranching are becoming significant drivers of deforestation. The majority of deforestation in the Amazon rainforest has taken place to make way for pastureland for cattle, with 80 percent of deforested land in Brazil used for cattle grazing. In addition to swidden agriculture, forest fires are also exacerbating deforestation in the region.

About one-third of the world's remaining rainforests, including a majority of the Amazon rainforest, are in Brazil. It is also the most biodiverse country on Earth, with more than 56,000 described species of plants, 1,700 species of birds, 695 amphibians, 578 mammals, and 651 reptiles (Butler, 2014). Brazil has experienced an exceptional level of deforestation over the past four decades. The construction of the Trans-Amazonian Highway, which opened large forest areas to development by settlers and commercial interests, accelerated deforestation in the early 1970s in the region. In more recent years, growing populations, combined with increased viability of intensive agricultural operations, have caused a further rise in forest loss. Historically, the majority of deforestation has resulted from the actions of poor subsistence farmers, but in recent decades this has changed, with a greater proportion of forest clearing done by large landowners and corporations (Butler, 2014). Indeed, the largest portion of deforestation is taking place owing to land clearing for commercial pasture and speculative interests. Direct drivers of deforestation are conversion of forests for pasture, farmland, and plantations, as well as surface mining, dams that inundate forested areas, and intense fires, whereas the indirect drivers of deforestation include subtler factors, like insecure land tenure, corruption, poor law enforcement, infrastructure projects, policies that favor conversion over conservation, and selective logging that creates the conditions for or enables activities that facilitate forest clearing (Butler, 2014).

In Argentina the drivers of deforestation and forest degradation have been identified as soybean crops, oil and gas exploitation, timber production, unsustainable grazing, and urbanization (Government of Argentina, 2010). In its REDD Preparation Proposal (R-PP) Argentina has also identified forest and grassland fires as major drivers of forest deforestation and degradation that result from other drivers. "The number and impact of fires increased over the last years, because of illegal land use and clearing of land for agricultural and livestock" (Government of Argentina, 2010). Not surprisingly, these drivers correlate directly to the country's top exports and global consumption demands. According to *The World Factbook*, Argentina's top exports are soybeans and derivatives, petroleum and gas, vehicles, corn, and wheat to Brazil (21.6 percent), China (7.3 percent), Chile (5.5 percent), and the United States (5.5 percent). Further fueling the drivers of forest deforestation and degradation is the country's high demand for more advanced farming technology to feed the demand for exports, which is clearly reflected in their top imports: machinery, motor vehicles, petroleum and natural gas, organic chemicals, and plastics from Brazil (33.2 percent), the United States (14.4 percent), China (12.4 percent), and Germany (4.7 percent). If this cycle is not broken, the future of forests in Argentina is bleak. Disrupting the cycle will require a change in global demand for soy products and gas or a shift in Argentina's economy away from these two main exports, but both of these solutions are unlikely to happen in the immediate future.

In Bolivia deforestation and forest degradation are happening in all the various ecoregions with varying degrees of severity. Bolivia acknowledges that there are several direct and indirect causes for forest degradation and deforestation. The main causes of deforestation and forest degradation include the expansion of agricultural lands, infrastructure development, forest fires, and illegal forest activities including logging (Government of Bolivia, 2010). Agricultural frontier expansion comes to be the primary cause of deforestation. It is directly linked to production of soybeans and other industrial crops by large-scale agro-industry (Government of Bolivia, 2010). Slash-and-burn practices are another type of agricultural deforestation in Bolivia, although this is considered minor compared to the large-scale agribusiness expansions. Infrastructure development is also considered one of the main direct causes of deforestation and forest degradation. Roads, gas pipelines, and urbanization require forest clearing as the first step for infrastructure development, and while Bolivian environmental law requires mitigation of negative environmental impacts, forest losses are generally not compensated. Forest fires and mineral extractions are also direct causes of deforestation. Indirect causes of forest loss are, unsurprisingly, directly related to Bolivia's economic situation and market demands. The foundation of the Bolivian economy is based on agriculture, forestry, hunting, and fishing (15 percent of the gross domestic product); mining and quarrying (14 percent); and manufacturing industries (19 percent) (Government of Bolivia, 2010). Bolivia's primary export commodities include natural gas, soybeans, crude petroleum, zinc ore, and tin to Brazil, the United States, and Japan (Economy Watch, 2010a). These top exports can be directly correlated to agricultural advancement, infrastructure development, and mineral extraction.

In Costa Rica the most significant drivers of deforestation are the establishment of agriculture and the raising of livestock (Government of Costa

Rica, 2010). This is the result of past development policies promoted by institutions like the Institute of Lands and Colonization, which later became the Agrarian Development Institute. Subsidized loans were given out as a result of these policies. The R-PP details specific forces that lead to deforestation and where they can be found. In protected wilderness areas, forest owners with unclear entitlement rights may not receive the benefits of the payment for ecosystem services scheme. In privately owned forests, restrictions on land-use change, over-regulation and administrative bans on sustainable forest management in primary and secondary forests, lack of access to a payment for ecosystem services scheme for forests under a forest management regime, inability of forest uses to compete with alternate uses, and a lack of enforcement may encourage deforestation. In indigenous reserves, insufficient revenue from forests and the inability of the state to sanction "irregular titling of land by squatters" contribute to deforestation. In national parks and biological reserves, the state's inability to control the threats presented by "squatters, illegal logging, hunters, and miners" has led to deforestation (Government of Costa Rica, 2010).

Drivers of deforestation in Africa

Africa as a continent is estimated to have contributed about 5.4 percent to the global loss of humid tropical forest during 2000–2005, compared to 12.8 percent in Indonesia and 47.8 percent for Brazil alone (Hansen et al., 2008). At the end of 1990, Africa had an estimated 528 million hectares, or 30 percent of the world's tropical forests. The rate of deforestation exceeded the global annual average of 0.8 percent in several sub-Saharan African countries. While commercial logging and cattle ranching are the main causes of deforestation in other parts of the world, the leading causes in Africa are associated with human activity (Agyei, 1998). Wood is the major energy source for cooking and heating in the continent. Conversion of forests for subsistence farming and commercial agriculture may account for as much as 60 percent of worldwide deforestation (Porter & Brown, 1991). Commercial logging is considered to be the cause of approximately 20 to 25 percent of annual disappearance of forests. The remaining 15 to 20 percent is attributed to other activities such as cattle ranching, cash crop plantations, and the construction of dams, roads, and mines (Porter & Brown, 1991). In Africa governments invest substantially more in cash crops than in food crops, as reflected in pricing and marketing policies. However, deforestation is primarily caused by the activities of the general population (Agyei, 1998).

In Cote d'Ivoire the most significant driver of deforestation is agriculture. The cash crops produced by Cote d'Ivoire are cocoa, coffee, rubber, palm oil, rice, and yams. The need for firewood is another driver of deforestation.

The country legally permits only the collection of deadwood for energy, but logging for firewood occurs regularly. The commercial logging of forests represents another driver. The country used to be a top exporter of wood in the 1960s and 1970s, but it seems that commercial logging exploitation is gradually falling. Bush fires, livestock agriculture, and mineral extraction are other direct drivers of deforestation (Republic of Cote d'Ivoire, 2014). According to the Cote d'Ivoire's R-PP, the indirect drivers of deforestation include the lack of a land management policy and weak governance. The land management policy was formulated in 1997 but has not been implemented yet. Lack of land security plays an important role in deforestation. Although the country tried to strengthen peasant ownership of land with the Land Law of 1998, it has accomplished little so far. Weak governance could be the cause of a ten-year internal conflict and a small budget, resulting in little control over the environmental and agricultural sectors. Increasing migration and population growth are also causing deforestation in Cote d'Ivoire. Indeed, the conflict from 2002 to 2009 contributed to deforestation through the plundering of forests, aggravation of land issues, and insecurity. Climate change has already proven to have an effect on the forests of Cote d'Ivoire as well as new infrastructure. These drivers were outlined in the R-PP (Republic of Cote d'Ivoire, 2014).

The drivers of deforestation and forest degradation in Kenya are also mainly agricultural expansion, cattle grazing, and human settlement. Kenyan economic policy provides incentives for horticulture and tourism, causing crop agriculture to expand. Expansion occurred mostly in areas with perennial water supplies. The extensive enclosure of riparian land along rivers and around swamps reduced wildlife's access to water. This caused many changes in their distribution and movement (Campbell et al., 2005). Many sources say that single factors such as population pressures or human encroachment through shifting cultivation cause deforestation. Others say it is due to an irreducible complexity (Campbell et al., 2005). Recent work suggests it is partially caused by illegal logging controlled by regional elites and corrupt government officials. Environmental organizations focus on good environmental governance or democratization as a check on deforestation (Klopp, 2012). De-gazetting of forestlands was an important driver of deforestation in the past, although the Forest Act 2005 seems to have addressed this now. Poor governance –including weak institutions, corruption, illegal logging, weak law enforcement, weak community participation in forest management, inadequate benefit sharing from forest resources, carelessness by local authorities, communal land systems and lack of private ownership of resources/land, unclear tenure and access to forest, and large-scale economic incentives for the exploitation of forest resources – is also causing deforestation in Kenya.

The Democratic Republic of the Congo (DRC) is at the heart of the Congo Basin, where the second-largest tropical forest in the world is located. Cognizant of the great potential for REDD Plus in the country, the DRC has forged ahead from the planning to the implementation stages of REDD Plus preparedness. According to Aquino and Guay (2013), available data on forest cover trends show an annual gross deforestation rate of 0.25 percent over the 1990–2000 period. Initial estimates for the 2000–2010 period suggest a rate of 0.23 percent per year with little interannual variation (Aquino & Guay, 2013). Although these deforestation rates are lower than the global average for tropical countries, they are relatively high for Central Africa, and high in absolute terms given the size of the DRC's total forest area. The DRC is among the ten countries with the largest absolute deforestation over the last decade: 3.7 million hectares of forest cover loss for the period 2000–2010 (Aquino & Guay, 2013). The DRC's forests face six major threats that drive deforestation: agriculture, pastureland, infrastructure/new settlements, mining extraction, firewood collection, and illegal logging. These are the results of, on one hand, the increasing market demand from a fast-growing internal and regional urban population, as well as the good prospects for international exports, with positive price projections for most of the commercial crops grown in the subregion, and, on the other hand, the large suitable land area that remains uncultivated (approximately 47 million hectares available for the production of palm oil) (World Bank, 2013). While it is fair to say that until now the deforestation rate has been passive because poor infrastructure has restricted land accessibility, the poor governance has not materialized the goal of preventing deforestation. A recent comprehensive study of the causes of deforestation suggests that, for the time being, the expansion of slash-and-burn agriculture is the most important direct cause of deforestation across the entire DRC, followed by small-scale fuelwood harvesting (Food and Agriculture Association-University College London, 2013).

Cameroon's forest is being deforested from logging, fuelwood collection, and subsistence farming (Nix, n.d.). In the recovery following the economic crisis caused by the devaluation of the CFA franc, building and public works projects increased domestic demand for timber products. Cameroon lacks an effective forest conservation program and suffers from endemic and pervasive corruption, giving rise to logging, which is highly damaging to the rainforest environment. According to published reports, the vast majority of logging companies operating in Cameroon are foreign owned and have aggressively and unsustainably logged their concessions without much concern over the local environment or prosecution by corrupt forestry officials (Butler, 2006a). Deforestation is beginning to have a significant environmental impact in parts of the country. In the north, deforestation has been blamed for increasing soil erosion, desertification, and reduced quality of pastureland, and overhunting and overfishing are a problem elsewhere in Cameroon (Butler, 2006a).

Why do these drivers exist?

The causes or drivers of deforestation are complex and vary within countries over time, from country to country as well as from region to region. In Asia commercial logging is most prominent, followed by cultivation of cash crops, particularly oil palm, biofuels, and small-scale agriculture (Matthews, 2002; Uryu et al., 2008). The increased demand for pulp in China and crude palm oil in Europe has been making the situation worse in recent years (Kaninnen et al., 2007). In Latin America expansion of pasturelands for cattle ranching and large- and small-scale farming, compounded by road construction, are the dominant drivers of deforestation (Barreto et al., 2000; Fearnside, 2005). Insecure property rights exacerbate the situation, although government policies have facilitated migration and subsidized agricultural production. "Distorted agrarian, forest and environmental policies, weak laws and regulations, insecure property rights not only over land, but also over timber, which allied to social and political factors, such as uneven distribution of land and strong organization of landless peasants, led to land conflicts and deforestation" (de Oliveira, 2008, p. 303). In the African region, commercial logging, wood collection for fuel and subsistence, and increasing cash crop farming have been the central causes of deforestation (Dessi & Kleman, 2007; Geist & Lambin, 2001). In addition, migration, population growth, a lack of forest policy enforcement, and mismanagement due to weak institutions are some of the dominant causes of deforestation in Africa.

While previous research has identified the drivers of deforestation, a comprehensive analysis of why countries have certain drivers of deforestation and forest degradation has not been completed. Many countries have identified their drivers of deforestation and forest degradation, but little research has been done to understand why such drivers exist and whether those drivers can be eliminated. In the last decade, over half of global forest and peatland destruction has taken place to meet increasing consumer demand for a few key commodities, including cattle products, palm oil, and soy. Some of the pressures behind the drivers of deforestation and forest degradation may come from other countries, specifically developed countries that want raw goods and materials from developing countries. Increasing global demands for everything from beef and leather shoes, apparel, and furniture to pet products have been intensifying cattle farming as well as deforestation. From soap to potato chips, palm oil is an ingredient in a wide spectrum of processed consumer products. Soy is used in a range of products from animal feed to protein shakes. These products find their way to the United States, Europe, and other advanced economies either directly or indirectly via other countries. For example, beef, palm oil, and leather products may have originated in Indonesia or Brazil, even if they are labeled "made in China" or "made in Italy."

The existing literature on forest management and REDD takes into consideration different levels of governance and ways to improve the management of forests and to mitigate climate change. The focus is getting governance right at the local project level. The idea of "getting the rules right" can be important, yet it remains insufficient for understanding the failure or success of REDD; therefore, we move beyond getting the governance system and the rules right in an individual developing country to examine the power that lies behind the international negotiations to address climate change and indirect drivers of forest loss. Getting the rules right in an individual developing country that is implementing REDD strategies may apparently provide some optimism that the forest is being protected to absorb more carbon dioxide to address the challenges of climate change. Examples also demonstrate that the money earned by selling the carbon storage is helping forest communities to diversify their sources of income by investing the money in alternative businesses. Many studies report these positive dimensions although they criticize the process of REDD policy making as not inclusive and suffering from democratic deficits (Pettenella & Brotto, 2012; Ojha et al., 2013). The studies argue that if the process is made inclusive, the problem of land tenure is addressed, and earnings are distributed equally among the stakeholders/members of the forest community, REDD can be implemented effectively and will be a very useful tool to mitigate GHG emissions to address climate change. Although these studies identify the drivers of deforestation, they have not done research to understand why these drivers of deforestation exist in the first place and the implications of these indirect drivers at local, national, and international stages to address the actual disease instead of symptoms of REDD or REDD Plus.

In order to understand this complex issue, the drivers of deforestation need to be divided into two categories: direct (or proximate) and indirect (or underlying) drivers. Direct causes are physical in nature and are connected to the actual process of deforestation. Examples include agricultural expansion, wood extraction, and infrastructure development such as roads, dams, human settlements, and urbanization. Indirect or underlying causes refer to circumstances or policies that drive the direct causes of deforestation. These include demographic, technological, policy or institutional, cultural, and economic forces. Much research focuses on either just one or a handful of direct drivers; therefore, it is difficult to get a clear picture of the drivers of deforestation and the actual utility of REDD (Contrearas-Hermosialla,

2000; UNFCCC, 2006). We focus on explaining why these indirect drivers exist and are connected to direct drivers of deforestation and forest degradation. The case studies of deforestation and forest degradation above clearly indicate that agriculture, logging, infrastructure development, cattle ranching, forest fires, human settlement, and firewood collection are the most commonly found drivers of deforestation. In Asia commercial agriculture, commercial logging, and human settlement are major drivers of deforestation. In Latin America commercial agriculture and commercial livestock production are the major causes of deforestation, and in Africa commercial agriculture, logging, and human settlement are major drivers of deforestation. An insightful analysis of these drivers envisions that except for human settlement due to population growth, other direct drivers are powerfully connected to the capitalist market system – the global supply and demand system of the neoliberal free market economy that believes in cornucopian economic growth.

In the capitalist global economy, the big multinational companies of the developed countries enter in developing countries in search of cheap raw materials, cheap labor, and lax environmental regulations to meet the rising demand for products in the rich countries and among rich people in poor countries as well. Prosperity for the few founded on environmental destruction, forest degradation, and persistent social injustice is no foundation for a civilized society (Jackson, 2011) and not an appropriate route to achieve the goals of REDD. Consumers play a vital role in influencing suppliers to adopt sustainability standards that reduce impacts on global forests, while benefiting local livelihoods and protecting ecosystems. Companies need to track the sources of the palm oil, beef, and leather ingredients in the products they market. By pledging support for sustainably produced commodities, consumers can assert positive pressure on companies to make changes in their supply chains and certify their raw materials did not come from areas of recent tropical deforestation.

The prosperity in industrialized countries that makes extensive meat eating possible facilitates a substantially more intensive form of food production than can be sustained in non-industrialized countries (Paterson, 2001). The ecological aspect of meat production contains two concerns: more throughputs of resources and more agricultural land. Seager (1993) noted that between 1960 and 1985, 40 percent of all Central American rainforests were cleared to create pasture for beef cattle and that cattle ranching is responsible for 85 percent of topsoil erosion in the United States, along with similar devastation in Australia and Canada. Fearnside (2005) argued:

> Amazonian deforestation rates have trended upward since 1991, with clearing proceeding at a variable but rapid pace. Although Amazonian forests are cut for various reasons, cattle ranching predominates. The

large and medium-sized ranches account for about 70% of clearing activity. Profit from beef cattle is only one of the income sources that make deforestation profitable. Forest degradation results from logging, ground fires (facilitated by logging), and the effects of fragmentation and edge formation. Degradation contributes to forest loss. The impacts of deforestation include loss of biodiversity, reduced water cycling (and rainfall), and contributions to global warming.

(p. 680)

The use of paper for facial tissues, paper napkins, disposable diapers, and paper shopping bags in the developed countries and among the pockets of rich people in developing countries has also been responsible for a forest cover loss of more than 13 million hectares in developing countries each year since 1990 (Brown, 2009). Biofuels have been promoted as a source of renewable energy that contributes to energy security, rural development, and GHG emissions reductions when compared to fossil-derived fuels. Many countries have now established targets for incorporating biofuels into the supply of transport fuel without considering the negative impacts this would have on the goals of sustainable development and agricultural practices. Biofuels come from oil palms, sugarcane, and soybeans, and there is serious concern that expansion of these feedstock crops could have negative impacts on forest conservation due to direct and indirect land-use change. Porter and Brown (1991) noted that conversion of forests for mainly commercial agriculture may account as much as 60 percent of worldwide deforestation.

Logging is one of the most serious aspects of deforestation and forest degradation. Commercial logging to meet the global rich's insatiable demand for woodwork and furniture accounts for more than one-quarter of the global deforestation problem. With a construction boom fueling demand for wood, the rate of logging in Africa, the Amazon, and Indonesia has increased. Despite improved logging techniques and greater international awareness of and concern for the rainforests, serious unsustainable logging of tropical rainforests continues through legal loopholes and illegal criminal syndicates (Butler, 2012b). Moreover, to address the concern about depleting timber stocks that could satisfy the increasing global timber demands of the neoliberal economy and free trade, timber operations are increasingly being replaced by monoculture plantation forestry, which is impoverishing biodiversity. Open international markets and cheaper communications costs have made some exotic raw materials and agricultural products affordable to consumers in developed countries. The growing reliance of agribusiness on oil palm and the needs of the paper industry are at the root of the immense deforestation of rainforests in Asia, Latin America, and Africa.

Deforestation and forest degradation are indirect but very prominent causes of the greenhouse effect. Estimated emissions from deforestation represent about 20 percent of the increased concentration of GHGs in the atmosphere. "Between 1990 and 2005, the world lost 3 percent of its forests. Some 200 km² of the forestland – twice the size of Paris – disappears each day. Globalization is often an ally of the chainsaw" (Huwart & Verdier, 2013, p. 114). Indeed, deforestation is primarily due to the conversion of forests into agricultural land, livestock production, and commercial logging in developing countries for the sake of raw materials and exports to keep these developing countries involved in the neoliberal market system and meet the demands of the consumer society. Agriculture, logging, and mineral extraction in developing countries are primarily export oriented. For example, "between 1996 and 2003, Brazilian soy exports to China rocketed from 15000 to 6 million tonnes. This dynamism involved deforestation and converting part of rainforest into farmland" (Huwart & Verdier, 2013, p. 114). Forests in Asia, Latin America and the Caribbean, and sub-Saharan Africa are being ravaged every day. The international markets and consumerist societies play a major insidious role in preventing REDD from achieving both climate mitigation and development. Research so far has examined forests and REDD policy instruments in developing countries as ways to address deforestation and reduce GHG emissions that result from deforestation and forest degradation. However, they seem to ignore the roles of free market economy, consumerism in developed countries, and scientific management of forests.

According to a comprehensive review report by the Working Group on Development and Environment in the Americas, the environmental impacts of trade liberalization and related economic reforms in Latin America suggest that, with some exceptions, free trade policies have taken a heavy toll on the environment (Working Group on Development and Environment in the Americas, 2004). Drawing on original research, the report found ample reasons to call into question the prevailing political assumptions that rapid integration into the world economy will automatically lead to environmental improvement. In addition to the serious challenges to the success of the REDD generated by international free markets, it suffers four fundamental problems: leakage, additionality, permanence, and measurement, which we discuss in detail in other chapters of this book. Without incorporating these issues into REDD policies, treating REDD as panacea is shortsighted and just equal to "greenwashing."

Conclusion

This chapter has provided an overview of the location of REDD projects and the direct and indirect causes of deforestation and forest degradation.

The chapter also analyzed the underlying causes of deforestation, linking the debate on deforestation and forest degradation to the global economy. Since the kick-off of REDD projects in 2008, developing countries in Asia, Africa, and Latin America and the Caribbean are either completing the R-PP phase or are implementing the full-scale REDD projects. In Asia and Latin America 16 countries on each continent are involved in REDD projects, whereas 24 countries in sub-Saharan Africa are involved.

The major drivers of deforestation and forest degradation are agriculture, collection of firewood, and logging in Africa and Asia, whereas in Latin America and the Caribbean cattle ranching and agriculture outstrip other causes. The analysis of these drivers demonstrates that apart from a small amount of deforestation for subsistence farming and fuelwood collection in developing countries, the primary cause of deforestation is export oriented, primarily driven by open free market systems. This chapter shows that unless serious efforts are made to change the functioning of the open market engine of the economy, the REDD projects will achieve little in addressing climate change; rather, they will accelerate leakage in forestry management.

References

Agyei, Y. (1998). Deforestation in sub-Saharan Africa. *African Technology Forum, 8*(1), 1–4. Retrieved from http://web.mit.edu/africantech/www/articles/Deforestation.htm

Aquino, A., & Guay, B. (2013). Implementing REDD+ in the Democratic Republic of Congo: An analysis of the emerging national REDD+ governance structure. *Forest Policy and Economics, 36*, 71–79.

Barreto, P., Nogueron, R., Souza Jr., C., Anderson, A., Salomao, R., & Wiles, J. (2000). *Human pressure on the Brazilian Amazon*. Washington, DC: World Resource Institute.

Bellassen, V., Crassous, R., Dietzsch, L., & Schwartzman, S. (2008). *Reducing emissions from deforestation and degradation: What contribution from carbon markets?* Caisse des Depots, Climate Report, no. 14. Paris: Mission Climate. Retrieved from http://www.cdcclimat.com/IMG/pdf/14_Etude_Climat_EN_Deforestation_and_carbon_markets.pdf

Brown, L. (2009). *Plan B 4.0: Mobilizing to save civilization*. New York, NY: Earth Policy Institute.

Butler, R. (2006a). Cameroon: Tropical rainforests. *Mongabay*. Retrieved from http://rainforests.mongabay.com/20cameroon.htm

Butler, R. (2006b). Papua New Guinea: Tropical rainforests. *Mongabay*. Retrieved from http://rainforests.mongabay.com/20png.htm

Butler, R. (2012a). Drivers of deforestation. *Mongabay*. Retrieved from http://rainforests.mongabay.com/deforestation_drivers.html

Butler, R. (2012b). Rainforest logging. *Mongabay*. Retrieved from http://rainforests.mongabay.com/0807.htm

Butler, R. (2014). Brazil: Rainforests. *Mongabay*. Retrieved from http://rainforests.mongabay.com/20brazil.htm

Campbell, D., Lusch, D., Smucker, T., & Wangui, E. (2005). Multiple methods in the study of driving forces of land use and land cover change: A case study of SE Kajiado district, Kenya. *Human Ecology, 33*(6), 763–794.

Central Intelligence Agency. (2015). *The world factbook*. Retrieved from https://www.cia.gov/library/publications/the-world-factbook/geos/print_ar.html

Contrearas-Hermosialla, A. (2000). *The underlying causes of forest decline*. Bogor, Indonesia: Center for International Forestry Research.

de Oliveira, Jose. (2008). Property rights, land conflicts and deforestation in the eastern Amazon. *Forest Policy and Economics, 10*(5), 303–315.

Dessi, G., & Kleman, J. (2007). Pattern and magnitude of deforestation in the south central Rift Valley region of Ethiopia. *Mountain Research and Development, 27*(2), 162–168.

Drollette, D. (2013, May 20). Plague of deforestation sweeps across South-east Asia. *The Guardian*. Retrieved from http://www.theguardian.com/environment/2013/may/20/deforestation-south-east-asia

Economy Watch. (2010a). *Bolivia trade, exports and imports*. Retrieved from http://www.economywatch.com/world_economy/bolivia/export-import.html

Economy Watch. (2010b). *Cambodia trade, exports and imports*. Retrieved from http://www.economywatch.com/world_economy/cambodia/export-import.html

Fearnside, P. (2005). Deforestation in Brazilian Amazonia: History, rates and consequences. *Conservation Biology, 19*(3), 680–688.

Foley, J. A., Asner, G. P., Costa, M. H., Coe, M. T., DeFries, R., Gibbs, H. K., . . . Snyder, P. (2007). Amazonia revealed: Forest degradation and loss of ecosystem goods and services in the Amazon Basin. *Frontiers in Ecology and the Environment, 5*(1), 25–32.

Food and Agriculture Organization-University College London. (2013). *Analysis of drivers of deforestation and forest degradation in DRC*. (Unpublished.)

Geist, H., & Lambin, E. (2001). *What drives tropical deforestation? A meta analysis of proximate and underlying causes of deforestation based on subnational case study evidence*. Louvain-la-Neuve, Belgium: LUCC International Project Office.

Government of Argentina. (2010). *Forest Carbon Partnership Facility (FCPF) readiness preparation proposal (R-PP)*. Retrieved from https://www.forestcarbonpartnership.org/sites/forestcarbonpartnership.org/files/Documents/PDF/Jun2010/Argentina_R-PP_June_2010_0.pdf

Government of Bolivia. (2010). *UN-REDD national joint programme document*. United Nations Collaborative Programme on Reducing Emissions from Deforestation and Forest Degradation in Developing Countries. Retrieved from http://www.un-redd.org/UNREDDProgramme/CountryActions/Bolivia/tabid/976/language/en-US/Default.aspx

Government of Costa Rica. (2010). *Readiness preparation proposal (R-PP)*. Retrieved from http://forestcarbonpartnership.org/costa-rica

Greenpeace. (n.d.). *The problems of deforestation in Asia*. Retrieved from http://www.greenpeace.org/eastasia/campaigns/forests/problems/

Hansen, M., Stehman, S., Potapov, P., Loveland, T., Townshend, J., Defries, R., . . ., DiMiceli, C. (2008). Humid tropical forest clearing from 2000 to 2005 quantified by using multitemporal and multiresolution remotely sensed data. *Proceedings of the National Academy of Sciences of the United States of America, 105*(27), 9439–9444.

Huwart, J.-Y., & Verdier, L. (2013). What is the impact of globalization on the environment? In Jean-Yves Huwart and Loïc Verdier (Eds)., *Economic globalization: Origins and consequences*, 108–125. Paris: Organisation for Economic Co-operation and Development. http://dx.doi.org/10.1787/9789264111905-8-en

Indrarto, G. B., Murharjanti, P., Khatarina, J., Pulungan, I., Ivalerina, F., Rahman, J., . . ., Muharrom, E. (2012). *The context of REDD+ in Indonesia: Drivers, agents and institutions*. Working Paper 92. Bogor, Indonesia: CIFOR.

Jackson, T. (2011). *Prosperity without growth? The transition to sustainable development*. Oxon, UK: Sustainable Development Commission.

Kaninnen, M., Murdiyarso, D., Seymour, F., Angelsen, A., Wunder, S., & German, L. (2007). *Do trees grow on money? The implications of deforestation research for policies to promote REDD*. Bogor, Indonesia: Center for International Policy Research.

Klopp, J. (2012). Deforestation and democratization: Patronage, politics and forests in Kenya. *Journal of Eastern African Studies, 6*(2), 351–370.

Mather, A. S., & Needle, C. L. (2000). The relationships of population and forest trends. *The Geographical Journal, 166*(1), 2–13.

Mather, R. (Ed.). (2012). *Preparing REDD in Vietnam, Lao PDR and Cambodia: Designing a REDD-compliant benefit distribution system*. Gland, Switzerland: International Union for Conservation of Nature.

Matthews, E. (Ed.). (2002). *The state of the forest: Indonesia*. Bogor, Indonesia: Forest Watch Indonesia and Global Forest Watch.

Meyer, W. B., & Turner, B. L. (1992). Human population growth and global landuse/land-cover change. *Annual Review of Ecology and Systematics, 23*, 39–61.

Ministry of Agriculture and Rural Development, Vietnam. (2014). *Emissions reductions program idea note (ER-PIN)*. Retrieved from https://www.forestcarbonpartnership. org/vietnam

Nix, S. (n.d.). Cameroon's rainforest. *About.com*. Retrieved from http://forestry. about.com/cs/rainforest/p/cameroon_rf.htm

Ojha, H., Ghimire, S., Pain, A., Nightingale, A., Khatri, D. & Dhungana, H. (2013). Carbon, community and governance: Is Nepal getting ready for REDD+? *Forests, Trees and Livelihoods, 22*(4), 216–229.

Paterson, M. (2001). *Understanding global environmental politics: Domination, accumulation, resistance*. New York, NY: Palgrave.

Pettenella, D., & Brotto, L. (2012). Governance features for successful REDD+ projects organization. *Forest Policy and Economics, 18*, 46–52.

Porter, G., & Brown, J. W. (1991). *Global environmental politics*. Boulder, CO: Westview.

Republic of Cote d'Ivoire. (2014). *Readiness preparation proposal (R-PP)*. Retrieved from https://www.forestcarbonpartnership.org/côte-divoire

Royal Government of Cambodia. (2008). *Readiness plan idea note (R-PIN): Submitted to the FCPF 2008*. Retrieved from http://theredddesk.org/sites/default/files/cambodia_r-pin.pdf

Seager, J. (1993). *Earth follies: Feminism, politics and the environment*. London: Earthscan.

United Nations Collaborative Programme on Reducing Emissions from Deforestation and Forest Degradation in Developing Countries (UN-REDD Programme). (2011). *Cambodia national UN-REDD national programme document*. Retrieved from http://www.un-redd.org/AboutUNREDDProgramme/NationalProgrammes/Cambodia/tabid/6896/Default.aspx

United Nations Framework Convention on Climate Change (UNFCCC). (2006). *Background paper for the workshop on Reducing Emissions from Deforestation in developing countries—Part II: Policy approaches and positive incentives*. Working Paper 1(b). Bonn: United Nations.

Uryu, Y., Mott, C., Foead, N., Yulianto, K., Budiman, A., Takakai, F., . . . Stüwe, M. (2008). *Deforestation, forest degradation, biodiversity loss and CO2 emissions in Riau, Sumatra, Indonesia*. Jakarta, Indonesia: WWF Indonesia.

Working Group on Development and Environment in the Americas. (2004). *Globalization and the environmental: Lessons from the Americas*. Washington, DC: Heinrich Böll Foundation. Retrieved from http://ase.tufts.edu/gdae/Pubs/rp/WorkingGroupExecSummary.pdf

World Bank. (2013). *Deforestation trends in the Congo Basin: Reconciling economic growth and forest protection*. Retrieved from http://elibrary.worldbank.org/doi/abs/10.1596/978-0-8213-9742-8

5 Capitalism and the global division of labor's impact on the drivers of deforestation

Introduction

Globalization is the word that is used to describe international trade patterns and other interactions between countries that have led to an intertwining of cultures, ideas, people, and markets. For some, globalization has been beneficial, but for others it has been harmful. This interaction is favorable to the expansion of the free market economy and the accumulation of wealth. It has made the movement of money and technology easier as well as goods made in remote places. Globalization has decreased the prices of some goods, making them easier to purchase. However, much of the expansion of wealth has been based on the accelerated use of natural resources, particularly in the less developed world. This includes the largest common-pool resource – air. It has also expanded the power of the wealthiest countries and some businesses to the detriment of the weaker countries and businesses. This expansion of power is reaching into how a number of countries govern their forests. Reducing Emissions from Deforestation and Forest Degradation (REDD) provides some control over how forests are used and managed to actors who are outside of the REDD country and of the groups who previously managed the forests. The groups who provided on-the-ground management include government agencies, forest dwellers and indigenous peoples, and timber companies, as well as other communities who depended on the forests. It is very important that the voices of these groups not be diminished because forests support the livelihood of roughly 25 percent of the world's population (Norman & Nakhooda, 2015). REDD, as an international program, skews the conversation toward keeping forests for carbon sequestration and sinks, and it ignores the more pertinent issue of decreasing the drivers of deforestation. This framing of the problem has led to more than 20 entities donating to over 80 recipients for REDD projects (Norman & Nakhooda, 2015). The largest donor countries are Norway, the United States, Germany, Japan, and the United Kingdom (Norman & Nakhooda, 2015). The recipient countries receiving the most money are Indonesia and Brazil.

In this chapter, we discuss how control over countries' forests is being given to outside actors and why that is detrimental, what role privatization and aid are playing in that loss of control, and how economies are linked between countries that are considered to be developed and less developed.

Market-based governance over the environment

There are multiple ways to regulate and address environmental problems. There is a continuum ranging from complete government control to absolute open access without any government regulations (Smith, 2013, p. 51). Neither extreme of the continuum exists in practice. Some mixture is used in each society. Sometimes a society relies more on market forces and less on government to provide a good or service that satisfies its needs (Savas, 2005). This is known as privatization, which is in the middle of the continuum. If privatization is simply defined as a "shift from government provision of functions and services to provision by the private sector" (Priest, 1988, p. 1), then those REDD projects that are participating in the market, in a sense, are a form of privatization because payments are received for carbon sequestration and storage. Carbon sequestration and storage are ecosystem services. It is becoming more common to pay for ecosystem services as a way to conserve natural resources. Ecosystem services consist of those parts of an ecosystem and its functions that are useful to humans. Examples include filtering of freshwater, vegetation and animal habitats, and recreation and ecotourism. A forest provides an ecosystem service when it sequesters and stores carbon along with providing a habitat for a variety of plant and animal species. The purpose of payment for ecosystem services (PES) is to make preserving the environment, or, more specifically, the services provided by the environment, more profitable than engaging in actions that cause environmental degradation. Payment is received for either conserving or enhancing ecosystem functions. REDD, as a PES scheme focused on deforestation and forest degradation, is supposed to make conserving forests and the services they provide more profitable than actions such as harvesting timber or clear cutting the land for agricultural use. It does this by placing a monetary value on the sequestration and storage of carbon.[1]

Protection of the environment and improved environmental quality are services traditionally provided by governments under command-and-control policies, which is a top-down approach in which the government dictates what must be done. Under command-and-control, people and organizations can face penalties for not following government orders. REDD is moving toward the use of private organizations and outside countries to provide some of those services and marks a direct shift away from command-and-control policies because market demand, rather than government force, is driving the change. It is doing this through PES and the carbon market.

Much of what has been written about REDD focuses on how to make the scheme viable and improve on it. There is also a large group that focuses on the protecting rights and ensuring that safeguards are implemented. While that literature is important, it misses a significant component of what is happening and will happen with REDD. Privatization and the move toward market-based governance must also be included in the analysis. The rise of the private sector to govern the environment has been referred to by many names, such as *free market environmentalism, non-state market-driven governance,* and *private environmental governance.* The common thread among all of these is the use of the private sector and the market to achieve desirable environmental goals. Some examples include sustainable forest certification, sustainable fisheries certification, and PES.

When the market is used to conserve the environment, there is still a role for government. That role is to enforce private property rights. According to this point of view, everything else can be left to market forces (Anderson & Leal, 2001). Free market environmentalism is based on "the positive incentives associated with prices, profits, and entrepreneurship" (Anderson & Leal, 2001, p. 4). This differs from "political environmentalism, which emphasizes negative incentives associated with regulation and taxes" (p. 4). In order to improve the quality of the environment, "a system of well-specified property rights to natural and environmental resources" must be in place (p. 4). Many REDD countries still need to clarify their property rights and who will receive the payments. Such a system is needed because it is assumed that property owners will make wise decisions about those resources since their wealth is at stake. In the case of REDD, that wealth would come from their decisions about managing the forest to optimize payments for emissions reductions. This viewpoint does allow for the holders of the property rights to be individuals, corporations, non-profit environmental groups, or communal groups. However, the owners are not the government, meaning that those resources cannot be public resources.

According to free market environmentalists, political (also understood as governmental) control of resources leads to waste and misuse. Ultimately, free market environmentalism is supposed to offer a win–win solution by sustaining economic growth while enhancing environmental quality. It uses market prices to "discipline consumers to allocate their scarce budgets among competing demands, and they discipline producers to conserve scarcer, higher-priced resources by finding substitutes that are less scarce" (Anderson & Leal, 2001, p. 163). The scarce resource is the ecosystem service provided by forests, carbon sequestration and storage.

The rise of non-government actors and the prominent role they play in environmental protection and conservation is referred to as *non-state market-driven governance*. This is the privatization of environmental protection. There are four characteristics of this type of governance (Cashore, 2002). First, the market is used to regulate sustainable products to meet the demand of customers. This assumes that rules and regulations are not followed based on state sovereignty demanding those rules and regulations. Instead, enforcement is the result of verifying compliance with sustainable practices in order to meet consumer demand. Compliance is verified through an audit process that does not involve the state; rather, it is done through third-party certification bodies. The market gains rule-making authority. Like in free market environmentalism, the governments are left to enforce contracts and delineate property rights; they are no longer the sole source of rule-making authority. Consumers demand products and services that are delivered by the market (Cashore, 2002). REDD projects follow this type of governance.

While non-state market-driven governance refers to the private sector, in the case of REDD it would be outside and non-state market-driven governance, meaning that both other countries and the private sector are driving the governance of a country's resources. As REDD projects become part of the carbon market, they will be part of this type of governance. REDD projects would rely on the carbon market to regulate the sustainable management of forests to enhance and maintain carbon sequestration and storage capacity. This capacity would be verified by third-party auditors. When REDD is fully implemented, it will rely on industrialized countries and the private sector to purchase carbon credits, which are bought and sold in the carbon market. If the market demands more storage and sequestration capacity, more REDD projects would be created. If the market demands decrease and the profitability of REDD projects dropped enough, the forests would be used in other profitable ways, mainly for cattle grazing, agricultural land, and timber extraction.

For REDD, there is some regulation, but the degree of regulation depends on the country where the scheme is taking place. Overall, countries participating in REDD will have much less control over their national forests. Under REDD, countries create plans that are to be implemented in local forests with broad guidelines for how REDD is to be achieved in that country. If the country is accessing funds through the United Nations, one of the World Bank's organizations, or a donor country, the plan must be approved by those entities before any start-up funds can be received. As for property rights, that is still a significant problem for REDD in many countries. Many countries still need to clearly delineate property rights. This is a contentious issue because the owner of the rights receives the profits derived from the REDD projects. Clear rights to land also mean legal standing if harm is done in the form of not receiving benefits or not being allowed to participate as a stakeholder in the decision-making process. Countries that are creating REDD projects often have tenuous land tenure systems, especially for indigenous peoples and other forest-dwelling communities. Usually the government has some form of ownership over the land, while the people using the land have usufructuary rights, which means they have the right to access and use the land and its resources but do not have a title to it or to profits derived from it. In addition to a clear land tenure system, there must be a clear allocation of rights to carbon. It is possible that forest dwellers, timber companies, or local governments have rights to the land and the profit from timber but that the national government maintains the rights to the carbon and thus to the profits derived from carbon credits. In these cases, who is entitled to receive REDD payments? The extent of vertical benefit sharing between countries and local stakeholders is a question that still needs to be addressed. How much money should be given to local stakeholders, and how much money should be kept to enhance governance and implement national REDD plans (Luttrell et al., 2012, p. 131)? There has been pressure on REDD countries to answer these questions. This is part of governance and another attempt to "get the rules right" by the architects of REDD. As you will see, this effort is futile in the long run for both sustainable development and mitigation of climate change.

Problems with REDD financial and funding schemes

The ways in which REDD is funded are problematic. There are two different types of funding. One type is bilateral and multilateral aid. The other is the carbon market, which mostly deals with the ongoing security of carbon credits once REDD projects have been developed. Each of these methods has its own set of problems, which are discussed below.

Funding REDD's start-up costs: bilateral and multilateral aid

The bulk of REDD funding to date has occurred through bilateral funding (the largest mechanism) and multilateral funding (Streck, 2012). Bilateral aid occurs between a single donor country and a single recipient country. Of all the donors in the bilateral category, Norway is the single largest source among countries that have actually given the aid. As shown in chapter 2, many donors have pledged large amounts but have distributed only a fraction of that amount. For example, donors have deposited only roughly 75 percent of what has been pledged to multilateral development banks for REDD (Norman & Nakhooda, 2015). REDD countries are receiving only a portion of what has been committed to them. One study tracked finances for seven REDD countries and showed that while roughly US$350 million was pledged, less than half of that amount was disbursed to the REDD countries (Canby et al., 2014). There is something even more troublesome. Only 12 percent of all multilateral funding that has been given by donors has been disbursed to REDD countries, whereas 32 percent of the money has been approved to be given out (Norman & Nakhooda, 2015). If the financing of REDD is done through bilateral aid, can donors provide enough aid to the developing countries? It is not likely that donors can cover this cost. At some point, REDD will have to rely mostly on the market. Multilateral aid is provided by a group of donor countries or an institution that receives money from multiple donor countries and is given to many recipient countries. The two largest multilateral donors are the Global Environment Facility and the Forest Carbon Partnership Facility. As stated in chapter 2, both are part of the World Bank, and the Forest Carbon Partnership Facility is in collaboration with the United Nations. Why do countries give money to fund REDD? What do donors get in return? Theoretically, they get the satisfaction of doing their part to help mitigate climate change, which will have a huge impact on future generations. Often, REDD money "was labeled as aid to help international donors reach aid targets" (Angelsen, 2013, p. 1). Another reason is that countries receive less pressure to reduce their emissions if they can prevent more emissions and increase the sink capacity in developing countries. If donors eventually go on to purchase emissions reduction credits, they get the right to continue polluting while other countries make the sacrifice of curbing emissions and not utilizing their forests. Some industrialized countries have an incentive to purchase offset credits because this is cheaper than reducing emissions from their own domestic sources. Many of the REDD countries lack the institutional capacity to administer REDD programs and must receive readiness funds to help them prepare. This involves a great amount of risk taking on the part of donors.

Carbon markets

Carbon markets have emerged as a seemingly viable method to mitigate climate change. The Clean Development Mechanism (CDM), a result of the 1997 Kyoto Protocol, helped establish the first carbon markets, such as Europe's Emissions Trading Scheme (ETS). The CDM, much like REDD, has twin goals of emissions reductions and sustainable development in the global South (Bohr & Dill, 2011). Carbon markets grew steadily from their inception until 2010 when the total value decreased from US$143.7 billion to US$141.9 billion (Linacre, Ambrosi, & Kossoy, 2011b, p. 9). The World Bank has been the major force driving carbon markets. According to a World Bank report, the regulated carbon market has contracted, but the voluntary carbon market has increased (Linacre, Ambrosi, & Kossoy, 2011). Proponents of carbon markets argue that they allow for continued economic growth while still making progress on the mitigation of climate change. Trading schemes like the ETS have been incredibly successful for developed countries, with great profits being made by private industry. For example, one study showed an increase in profitability by €800 million for UK power generators owing to a lack of regulation that allowed generators to pass-through all marginal costs onto the market value of power (Milne, 2006). Carbon markets have been called "the world's biggest market overall" with "volumes comparable to credit derivatives inside a decade" (Kanter, quoted in Lohmann, 2009, p. 167). The combined worth of global emissions trading schemes is around US$30 billion (World Bank, Climate Change, 2014, p. 15).

Opponents of carbon markets argue that these carbon trading schemes allow participating entities to avoid taking responsibility for past actions and do not cut emissions at their source (McAfee, 2012, p. 110). One technicality of carbon markets, like that established by the CDM, is that accomplishing global emissions reduction requires that offsets be purchased from participants who can prove additionality. This is the amount of emissions reductions that occur above and beyond a business-as-usual scenario. The problem is that there is not a single agreed-on method for determining baselines for the business-as-usual scenario. The calculation of offsets can change greatly based on the method chosen. The variety of calculation methods means more conservative calculations lead to less additionality, while more generous ones can lead to more profits because of the greater amount of additionality. This opens up the potential for data that is inaccurate, at best, and for fraudulent manipulation that results from corruption, at worst. For projects selling the offsets, there is more pushback to use only the calculation methods that lead to greater additionality and thus greater profits. However, these generous calculations may mean that no real offsets are being provided. Not only have carbon trading schemes not achieved their goal of net emissions reductions, but they have not achieved their goal of sustainable development in the global South (Bohr & Dill, 2011, p. 407). Despite immense profits, the ETS has not been linked to any additional emissions reductions owing to a lack of evidence that purchased offsets have produced any additional emissions reductions (McAfee, 2012, p. 112).

While carbon markets are largely seen as a deficient method for addressing climate change, the World Bank is continuing to promote their use. In December 2011 at the Durban Climate Change Conference, the World Bank announced two new financial initiatives. The Carbon Initiative for Development is meant to help developing countries access carbon finance by supporting low-carbon energy efficiency (Carbon Initiative for Development,

2015). The third tranche of the BioCarbon Fund is meant to support the sequestration and storage of carbon in forests and agricultural land. There are some REDD projects in this fund. Both of these funds use carbon markets to address climate change and poverty alleviation.

REDD is exchanged through the over-the-counter (OTC) (or voluntary) market (World Bank, Carbon Finance Unit, 2011, p. 54). It makes up a significant amount of the OTC market. The first REDD carbon offsets to enter the voluntary carbon market came from a project in Kenya in 2011. The project created 1.16 million offsets and is set up to be a 30-year project (Linacre, Ambrosi, & Kossoy, 2011, p. 58). REDD credits were the fastest-growing sector of the carbon market. From 2009 to 2010, REDD's market share grew over 500 percent (p. 54). The voluntary carbon market refers to the market for carbon that functions outside of the compliance market. The trading volume is much smaller in comparison to the compliance market because demand is generated through voluntary efforts. In a compliance market, demand is generated through mandates and regulations. The voluntary carbon market lacks rules and regulations, which means it also lacks quality control.

Privatization and non-state market-driven governance

Should we be concerned about this shift toward privatization and non-state market-driven governance? The simple answer is yes. Carbon is being commodified as a way to make profits and solve an international environmental problem. While this is inherently not a problem, such commodification is leading to another form of colonialism, and there is still little evidence that it leads to actual emissions reductions. Another problem with using the market is that, in some cases, it may be more profitable to convert the forest than to conserve it and sell the carbon credits. One study found that converting a forest to palm oil production is more profitable than conservation for REDD (Butler, Koh, & Gazoul, 2009). In addition, if corporations do not receive some type of gain, they can stop purchasing carbon credits and, even worse, stop participating in REDD. We anticipate that this will happen given the current configuration of REDD. This brings up the issue of permanency. In order to operate successfully as a tool to assist in mitigating climate change, REDD projects need long-term funding. This can come either in the form of aid given to them or through selling of carbon credits in the market.

Transparency

How can the international community ensure that REDD is achieving its environmental goals? Many entities investing in REDD lack transparency, which makes it difficult to hold them accountable for the desired results. Many non-state actors, i.e. the private sector, are not as transparent as most governments. Corporations do not have to provide information that is requested by the public. However, many governments and some large international organizations such as the United Nations do provide information when it is requested.

There are actually many definitions that governments, businesses, and people use when they claim to be transparent, and many are not transparent at all, regardless of the claims they make. Some define transparency as providing data about their outcomes, while others define it as being open about everything from their decision-making process to their outcomes. There are also different types of transparency ranging from availability of information to the ability to request information that is easy for different groups to understand (Fung, 2013). According to Fung (2013) there are three types of transparency: freedom of information, open government, and targeted transparency. Freedom of information requires a government or organization to be transparent after a request has been made for information that is already possessed (p. 187). Open government is transparency through "the proactive dissemination of information" that is already possessed (p. 188). Targeted transparency occurs when people have the right to "compel organizations . . . to disclose information in order to advance some specific public purpose" (p. 189). The information may not be currently possessed, but the organization would be compelled to collect data that could provide the requested information. Targeted transparency is a prerequisite for achieving democratic transparency because it helps to hold accountable and regulate large organizations.

It is widely accepted that transparency is highly desirable for governments, businesses, and organizations. Transparency is crucial for achieving equity and holding entities accountable (Ramkumar & Petkova, 2007, p. 283). It allows more participation in decision-making processes. People can access the decision-making process better when they can formulate opinions based on actual data and previous decisions that have been made. They can be more active participants in the process rather than outside observers. Active participation is especially important for decisions about natural resources since many people depend on them for their livelihoods (Ramkumar & Petkova, 2007, p. 286). This reliance on natural resources is found in REDD countries. Such participation in decision-making processes can empower people through information disclosure (Florini, 2007, p. 3). The ability of all local stakeholders to participate helps them to ensure that their rights are protected and their voices are heard about the REDD projects. Unless REDD countries have some system for transparency, the participation and resource rights of communities who complete on-the-ground work for the REDD projects will be curtailed or non-existent (Lyster, 2011, p. 126). Moreover, transparency can promote efficient and effective policies by providing feedback about what works and what does not from people who are involved in implementation (Florini, 2007, p. 2).

It is important for REDD countries to be transparent for many reasons. First, donors and international organizations need to know that the projects are performing as expected. Monitoring systems must be transparent in order to ensure that implementation is occurring as expected and results are being achieved as well as to examine how REDD impacts the rights and livelihoods of forest dwellers (Luttrell, Loft, Gebara, & Kweka, 2012). Transparent monitoring systems provide assurance to donors and those purchasing carbon credits that carbon sequestration and storage is actually taking place. It is important to understand how REDD impacts forest dwellers. If that impact is negative, changes in governance and implementation must be made. Monitoring systems must also be transparent to assure donors and those purchasing carbon credits that the reductions are actually taking place. Given the remoteness of many REDD projects, without transparency it is difficult to ensure that benefit sharing with forest dwellers and others who utilize forests for their livelihoods is taking place.

Second, transparency helps to reduce corruption (Vatn & Vedeld, n.d., p. 12). It is important to know whether actual carbon sequestration and storage are taking place beyond a "business-as-usual" scenario. Without the availability of certified information, there could be fabricated trades, or carbon sequestration and storage that occurs only on paper and not through the enhancement of the forest itself. This makes Measurement, Reporting, and Verification mechanisms a very integral part of REDD should the market mechanism or aid money from other governments be used. A similar problem with corruption stems from illegal logging. Many of the REDD countries must deal with significant impacts from illegal logging. Sometimes the illegal logging takes place and government officials have no knowledge of it. In this case, corrupt acts have not occurred. In other cases, government officials may accept bribes to allow the logging to take place under the table, to speed up a permit, or to ignore overharvesting of timber (cutting an amount beyond what is permitted). These are acts of corruption. In either case, Measurement, Reporting, and Verification systems must be able to account for such activities. That information must then be made available so that the REDD country can be held accountable, emissions credits can be reduced if needed, or governments that provided aid can withhold further aid if they wish. The United Nations Collaborative Programme on Reducing Emissions from Deforestation and Forest Degradation in Developing Countries (UN-REDD Programme) provided support for some of its REDD partner countries to assess their corruption risks and create plans to address those risks. It is an element of successful governance (Lyster, 2011).

There are yet other reasons why transparency is needed. Transparency from international organizations is important because it allows donors and the broader public to know whether the goals of REDD are being reached and whether climate change is being mitigated. For REDD countries, transparency from the international organizations that provide them with money is important because they know what they can expect, how other REDD countries are doing, and how they fit into the overall scheme. It provides a way for the stakeholders to hold both the organizations and the REDD countries accountable. Openness from REDD countries allows everyone to follow exactly how the money is being spent.

The developed and less developed world

Now we shift to a larger perspective regarding privatization and non-state market-driven governance. Decreasing the role of national governments, removing regulations, and allowing the market to govern causes some countries to prosper while others are left less developed. If you examine different countries and their economies, it becomes apparent that some countries are more industrialized and developed than others. Industrialization and development exist on a continuum. Some countries have stronger economies, experience more economic growth overall, are wealthier, and tend to have the most advanced technology. They are considered developed. Some examples are the United States, the United Kingdom, and Norway. Other countries appear to be the exact opposite. They are not as industrialized, have less advanced technology, and experience slower economic growth, and, as a whole, their population is poorer. These countries are considered to be in the process of developing. There are some countries that are in the middle of the continuum, with varying degrees of technology and power. Examples of these countries are China and India.

This relationship of developed and developing countries is the source of an economic hierarchy that exists among countries. This hierarchy also depicts different levels of power. The countries at the bottom of the hierarchy are economically dependent on the countries at the top of the hierarchy. A country is dependent when its economy is "conditioned by the development and expansion of another country," which then places the dependent country in a "backward position exploited by the dominant countries" (Viotti & Kauppi, 1999, p. 349). The developed and dependent countries trade with one another. Both need to sell their goods. However, the trading does not take place on completely equal terms.

The more powerful countries and corporations exploit the weaker countries. That hierarchy also explains the flow of natural resources from one country to another. In many cases, the dependent country relies on the exportation of cash crops to support its economy and people. These cash crops can include timber as well as other agricultural products such as soybeans and rice. For example, Japan provides aid to Indonesia and the Philippines to secure imports of natural resources that Japan does not have. In some countries, deforestation is occurring because timber is a major export. In other areas, deforestation and forest degradation occur because agricultural land is expanded into forests in order to grow cash crops for export. The countries that export timber and agricultural products are dependent on the importing countries for their economic stability and their ability to obtain the finances needed to import goods they do not produce. This may seem fine if the exchange is equal. An equal exchange could be country A exporting soy to country B and then importing bananas from country B. Soy and bananas are relatively similar in price. However, that is not the exchange that takes place. A more realistic exchange is that country A is exporting soy to country B and importing vehicles or refrigerators from country B. How much soy does country A need to produce in order to obtain vehicles? How many vehicles does country B have to export to obtain the amount of soy it needs? The answer is that country B needs to produce considerably less than what country A has to produce to obtain its needed goods.

The above is a very simplified example. In reality, the less developed country trades with multiple developed countries, but at a cost to its own environment. This is often called *unequal ecological exchange* (Jorgenson, 2006). Unequal ecological exchange focuses on the patterns of trade and environmental harms. Specifically, trade patterns lead to certain environmental and ecological harms because developed countries treat less developed countries as sources of natural resources and agricultural goods, areas for waste disposal, and sinks for their global air pollution (Jorgenson, 2009).

The cause of dependence has two interrelated factors. First, the developed countries and transnational corporations own land and factories in the less developed countries to extract the additional value, that is, the profit, that the land and factories produce. Second, unequal exchange occurs, with the less developed countries exchanging cheaper goods (as in the above example of exchanging soy for vehicles or refrigerators) (Peet & Hartwick, 2009). What does this mean in the context of REDD? Ownership of carbon sequestration and sinks (through the purchase of credits) is similar to owning land because carbon has been turned into a commodity. The forests in REDD countries have been mainly used for exporting timber or expanding agricultural land to grow crops (Lambin & Geist, 2006). These products can be grown and exported because there is a demand for them as well as for timber. What happens when the forest becomes a REDD project and the demand for timber or crops does not go away? As we saw in a previous chapter, leakage occurs. Deforestation and forest degradation are shifted or intensified in other areas that are not part of a REDD project. These same forests are now being exploited for their capacity to sequester and store carbon. Limitations can be placed on how the forests are used to ensure that such capacity is maintained. This is problematic because communities often depend on forests for their livelihoods, including meeting their basic needs for food and fuel.

Countries in a position to provide aid have power over the countries that need the aid. While the donor country may not directly own the land, they can, and often do, place stipulations on how the aid is to be used. Bilateral funding contributes to dependency by the donor country and forces change to occur in order for the REDD country to receive the aid. If a country wants to receive bilateral aid, it must work with the donor country to change how its forests are managed and used in order to receive money for REDD activities. The balance of power is in favor of the donor country and the stipulations it places on the REDD country in order for it to receive the aid. Multilateral funding is also problematic. In this case, the organization, and not just a single country, has power over the REDD country if aid is to be given. Both policies and forest management practices must be changed for aid to be received. For both bilateral and multilateral aid, the acceptable policies and the ways they are to be implemented are heavily influenced by the donors. To ensure that implementation happens accordingly, a reporting and verification process by a third party takes places. Essentially, a country must stop using its forests in order to preserve and enhance their carbon sequestration and storage capacity. What happens while this is taking place? How does the REDD country recoup those lost funds? In most cases, the amount of aid does not cover the forgone profits. The REDD countries must do the bulk of the work and undergo much transformation, while the donor countries and corporations continue with business-as-usual operations.

Once aid has been received and REDD projects are developed, it is intended that the market and private investment will take over. This is done by placing a price on carbon. There are multiple ways to place a price on carbon. The two main tools are carbon taxes and emissions trading schemes. Others include offsets and results-based financing (Lacoq & Capoor, 2005). REDD is not a carbon tax; it is concerned with emissions trading schemes and results-based financing. It will be part of the larger category of emissions trading schemes. Some REDD projects are already participating in the voluntary carbon market, but there are not any national program-level participants (p. 43). It has also been proposed to create a separate carbon market (emissions trading scheme) for REDD.

A carbon tax adds a cost for all carbon emissions. It works to reduce emissions by forcing polluters to pay a flat rate for what they emit. If polluters cannot pay for all of their emissions or if it is cheaper to alter their operations to decrease emissions, they will scale back the amount they emit. Under a tax scheme, there is no limit on the amount of pollution allowed. Each emitter must pay for each unit of carbon emitted, and they are free to emit as much as they can afford. An emissions trading scheme sets a total amount of emissions that are allowed within the area. Each emitter must then have a permit for each ton of carbon they release. The number of permits is determined by the total amount of emissions allowed, which forces an argument to set a higher cap. Polluters must either cut back their emissions to the amount for which they hold permits, or purchase permits from other emitters who have scaled back their emissions. This is why emissions trading schemes are sometimes referred to as *cap-and-trade*. The price of a permit is flexible; it is based on what an emitter is willing to pay for a permit as well as the supply of permits and the demand for them. This makes the price of carbon and permits subject to market cycles.

That brings us to another aspect of dependency, price volatility. It is believed that less developed countries suffer from price volatility for products, mainly the raw goods they export. Overall, the prices have a downward tendency, meaning the price for the goods falls. The underdeveloped countries tend to sell their goods at prices below their value because the price does not reflect the labor used to produce the goods. This is in contrast to the stable prices for goods that experience gradual increases, such as the manufactured and finished products that are exported by developed countries.

The carbon market has experienced volatility, and the price for carbon offsets is now quite low. The height of the carbon market was in 2011, and it has steadily declined since that year (Norman & Nakhooda, 2015, p. 35). The price of carbon varies based on the country and the carbon pricing tool being used. It ranges from a low of US$1/tCO$_2$ to US$168/tCO$_2$ (World Bank, Climate Change, 2014, p. 32). Overall, the average price of carbon in emissions trading schemes is lower than the average amount paid under a carbon tax (p. 33). While REDD was experiencing huge growth in the voluntary carbon market in 2009, by 2012 the average price for forestry offsets began to decline. These prices have been declining because of increasing supply and a decreasing demand for the offsets. "In early 2014, the average bid and offer for issued credits was US$5–6/tCO$_2$e. Almost all project-level REDD emission reductions are currently transacted in the voluntary carbon market, but they are characterized by heterogeneity of demand, high price variability, and lack of transparency" (p. 43).

The idea of unequal exchange comes into play because the carbon credits are not worth very much if the market is volatile and the price is continuously dropping. This means that the credits are cheap because they are readily available and there are more than enough to meet the demand. Overall, REDD credits on the carbon market are still relatively new and small, but so far we can see some of the volatility that can be expected to take place on a larger scale.

This dependency is the result of globalization and the capitalist economy. The primary goal of capitalism is profit accumulation, which is accomplished through the selling of goods and services. REDD is an attempt to accumulate profit while benefiting the environment through the mitigation of climate change. Much of this profit accumulation is the result of exploiting both people and the environment, especially in less developed countries. Historically, the exploitation took place under colonialism, when some countries were considered colonies and used for their natural resources and cheap labor. Capitalism creates a constant state of dependence by exploiting the natural resources and cheap labor found in some countries. Remember that much of the labor that is being done in REDD countries is not being compensated. In many cases, countries must conduct studies to identify the state of their forests, and they must pass policies to begin implementation. Both are labor and technology intensive. This is often done with only US$200,000 made available for preparation activities, in the form of "readiness grants." The amount of aid that has been promised is quite different from the amount that has actually been given. Only a fraction of promised aid has been received.

Conclusion

Is the market better equipped to address environmental problems? Sometimes the market can handle environmental concerns, but these cases are limited. In the United States, much of the waste management for cities and town is privatized. One company will oversee a small city, and in some cases a few companies may have contracts for waste management in larger cities. The point is that these are small-scale situations with defined boundaries for a tangible service. There is a definite schedule for things like trash pick-up and deliveries to the landfill. It does not suffer from problems of leakage, additionality, and permanence.

The United States has utilized the market to control air pollution, but in many respects command-and-control has not disappeared. Emissions trading schemes were developed in areas that were considered to be in nonattainment of the standards set by the Clean Air Act. In many cases, these schemes did not lead to any net reduction in air pollution, and they created a right to pollute for the purchasers of the credits. Markets emerged for selling and buying emissions reductions credits, and in some cases these were full-time jobs for companies that were not complying with air quality standards. An even worse scenario is the Chicago Climate Exchange, which eventually shut down after its legally binding term ended in 2010. Another term was not started because carbon prices dropped drastically and companies stopped participating because carbon became a worthless commodity.

What does this mean for REDD?

REDD is being promoted as part of the green economy. A green economy is supposed to be different from our current economy because its outcomes are improved human well-being, social equity, and improved environmental quality (UN-REDD Programme, 2013a). In addition, a green economy is supposed to include all sectors of society. From this perspective, REDD, as part of the green economy, is completely the opposite of the interactions described above that created dependency and furthered poverty in some countries. REDD, in this light, is a path to development that is also sustainable for the environment. Globalization, and increased international trade, is promoted as a way to promote better ideals for everyone. Countries can trade based on their comparative advantage, meaning they trade the goods that they are best able to provide at a cheaper cost than everyone else. For less developed countries, this would mean decreasing their deforestation and forest degradation while increasing their capacity to store and sequester carbon. What could be bad about a scenario like that? According to the United Nations, REDD fits perfectly within the green economy (UN-REDD Programme, 2013a).

REDD has become another way to keep countries dependent and reliant on more powerful countries. It has also become a form of privatization because in some cases corporations are sponsoring REDD projects, donating money to entities to funnel to REDD projects, or will be expected to purchase carbon credits once they become available. Taking bilateral and multilateral aid into consideration, along with the use of the market, many actors outside of a country's government are now able to have a voice and decision in how that country oversees and uses its forests. These actors are corporate lobbies, multilateral banks, conservationist non-governmental organizations, and other countries. Technically, a country has sovereignty over how it governs and uses or chooses not to use its resources. However, some amount of sovereignty is given up when it decides to participate in REDD. You could say that the country should just choose to not participate, but then they are faced with the problem of not participating as much in climate mitigation and using their forests for timber or clear cutting them for the production of crops. Neither choice seems to be a good one. Rather, it's the old adage of choosing the lesser of two evils.

If REDD utilizes the carbon market, it is supposed to provide a win–win–win path. The first win is global efficiency gains because areas that can decrease the amount of carbon released into the atmosphere while increasing their sequestration capacity will participate in REDD (Lacoq & Capoor, 2005, p. 9). The second win is sustainable development for those countries participating in REDD. The third win is mitigation of climate change, which is an international benefit to everyone on the planet. One could even say that there is a fourth win in there with the idea that REDD Plus is now promoting the conservation of biodiversity, but at this point we'll stop at three.

While REDD has the potential for delivering many benefits, it is also riddled with significant problems that will prevent many of those benefits from being achieved. One problem is funding REDD without causing undue harm. On one hand, without funding from compliance carbon markets, it remains doubtful whether REDD could compete with the profits of alternative land uses such as oil palm plantations (Butler, Koh, & Gazoul, 2009, p. 71). On the other hand, relying purely on funding from other countries could lead to donor fatigue, resulting in inconsistent funding in the future (Streck, 2013). Inconsistent funds could have significant consequences for conservation projects like REDD that rely on consistent funding to compete with alternative land uses. Both carbon markets and funding from other governments are riddled with the problems described above.

A second and very significant problem with using emissions trading is that unless there is a global cap on emissions, the carbon market is pointless and will not play a role in mitigating climate change. At the time of this writing, there is no global cap on emissions trading. This makes the entire carbon market idea useless for climate change. It does, however, allow for money to be made in developing countries and for entities purchasing the credits to claim they are doing their part to battle climate change.

In the next chapter we examine whether or not REDD will help partner countries achieve economic growth, which is another goal of the program.

Box 5.1 The green economy

The green economy is a term used to describe a multitude of ways to achieve ecologically sound economic growth along with poverty alleviation. The economy is embedded within the environment. The environment provides the inputs for economic growth as well as absorbs its outputs, or waste. In general, economic growth has been based on the exploitation and overpollution of the environment. An example would be the early industrial revolution, which caused immense releases of greenhouse gases along with water pollution and heightened use of fossil fuels and overconsumption of renewable natural resources. The green economy is a way to avoid these ecological harms. The green economy is multifaceted. It can include renewable energy production and electric energy distribution, energy efficiency and storage, organic agriculture, greatly increased use of mass transportation or methods of alternative transportation, energy-efficient buildings, use of biofuels, carbon capture and storage, and payment for ecosystem services.

Note

1 It is important to remember that not all REDD projects are participating in the carbon market. Most are still in the early stages, with plans to participate in the carbon market once they are fully functioning.

References

Anderson, T. L., & Leal, D. R. (2001). *Free market environmentalism.* New York, NY: Palgrave.

Angelsen, A. (2013). *REDD as performance based aid.* World Institute for Development Economics Research Working Paper No. 2013/135. Retrieved from https://www.wider.unu.edu/publication/redd-performance-based-aid

Bohr, J., & Dill, B. (2011). Who benefits from market-based carbon mitigation. *Perspectives on Global Development and Technology, 10*, 406–428.

Butler, R. A., Koh, L. P., & Gazoul, J. (2009). REDD in the red: Palm oil could undermine carbon payment schemes. *Conservation Letters, 2*(2), 67–73.

Canby, K., Silva-Chavez, G., Breitfeller, J., Lanser, C., Norman, M., & Schaap, B. (2014). Tracking REDD finance: 2009–2012—finance flows in seven REDD countries. *Forest Trends: REDDX.* Retrieved from http://reddx.forest-trends.org/page/resources

Carbon Initiative for Development. (2015). *About us.* Retrieved from http://www.ci-dev.org/about-us

Cashore, B. (2002). Legitimacy and privatization of environmental governance: How non-state market-driven (NSMD) governance systems gain rule-making authority. *Governance, 15*(4), 503–529.

Florini, A. (Ed.). (2007). *The right to know: Transparency for an open world.* New York, NY: Columbia University Press.

Fung, A. (2013). Infotopia: Unleashing the democratic power of transparency. *Politics and Society, 41*(2), 183–212.

Höhne, Niklas, Klein, N., Gilbert, A., Lam, L., Toop, G., Wu, Q., . . . Wong, L. (2015). *State and trends of carbon pricing: 2014.* Washington, DC: International Bank for Reconstruction and Development/World Bank.

Jorgenson, A. K. (2006). Unequal ecological exchange and environmental degradation: A theoretical proposition and cross-national study of deforestation, 1990–2000. *Rural Sociology, 71*(4), 685–712.

Jorgenson, A. K. (2009). The sociology of unequal exchange in ecological context: A panel study of lower-income countries, 1975–2000. *Sociological Forum, 24*(1), 22–46.

Lacoq, F., & Capoor, K. (2005). *State and trend of the carbon market 2005.* Retrieved from https://wbcarbonfinance.org/docs/CarbonMarketStudy2005.pdf

Lambin, E. F., & Geist, H. J. (2006). *Land-use and land-cover change: Local processes and global impacts.* Heidelberg, Germany: Springer.

Linacre, N., Ambrosi, A., & Kossoy, P. (2011). *State and trends of the carbon market 2011.* World Bank, Carbon Finance Unit. Retrieved from http://siteresources.worldbank.org/INTCARBONFINANCE/Resources/StateAndTrend_LowRes.pdf

Lohmann, L. (2009). Regulatory challenges for financial and carbon markets. *Carbon & Climate Law Review, 3*(2), 161–171.

Luttrell, C., Loft, L., Gebara, M. F., & Kweka, D. (2012). Who should benefit and why? Discourses on REDD benefit sharing. In A. Angelsen, M. Brockhaus, W. D. Sunderlin, & L. V. Verchot, (Eds.), *Analyzing REDD: Challenges and choices*, 129–152. Bogor Barat, Indonesia: CIFOR.

Lyster, R. (2011). REDD, transparency, participation and resource rights: The role of law. *Environmental Science and Policy, 14*(2), 118–126.

McAfee, K. (2012). The contradictory logic of global ecosystem services markets. *Development and Change, 43*(1), 105–131.

Milne, R. (2006). "Windfall" claim fury. *Utility Week, 24*(23), 4.

Norman, M., & Nakhooda, S. (2015). *The state of REDD finance.* Center for Global Development, Working Paper 378. Retrieved from http://ssrn.com/abstract= 2622743

Peet, R., & Hartwick, E. (2009). *Theories of development: Contentions, arguments, alternatives* (2nd edition). New York: The Guilford Press.

Priest, G. L. (1988). Introduction: The aims of privatization. *Yale Law and Policy Review, 6*(1), 1–5. Retrieved from http://digitalcommons.law.yale.edu/cgi/viewcontent.cgi? article=1607&context=fss_papers.

Ramkumar, V., & Petkova, E. (2007). Transparency and environmental governance. In A. Florini (Ed.), *The right to know: Transparency for an open world*, 279–308. New York, NY: Columbia University Press.

Savas, E. S. (2005). *Privatization in the city: Success, failures, lessons.* Washington, DC: CQ Press.

Smith, Z. A. (2013). *The environmental policy paradox* (6th edition). Upper Saddle River, NJ: Pearson.

Streck, C. (2012). Financing REDD: Matching needs and ends. *Current Opinion in Environmental Sustainability, 4*(6), 628–637.

Streck, C. (2013). The financial aspects of REDD+: Assessing costs, mobilizing and dispersing funds. In R. Lyster, C. Mackenzie, & C. McDermott, (Eds.), *Law, tropical gorests, and carbon.* New York: Cambridge University Press.

United Nations Collaborative Programme on Reducing Emissions from Deforestation and Forest Degradation in Developing Countries (UN-REDD Programme). (2013a). *REDD in a green economy.* Retrieved from http://www.unredd.net/ index.php?option=com_docman&task=doc_download&gid=10815&Itemid=53

United Nations Collaborative Programme on Reducing Emissions from Deforestation and Forest Degradation in Developing Countries (UN-REDD Programme). (2013b). *Sharing national experiences in strengthening transparency, accountability and integrity for REDD.* Retrieved from http://nr.iisd.org/news/un-redd-explores-transparency-and-accountability-in-redd/

Vatn, A., & Vedeld, P. (n.d.). Governance structures for REDD: What will the solutions be? Under review with *Global Environmental Change.* Retrieved from http://www.isee2012.org/anais/pdf/sp29.pdf

Viotti, P. R., & Kauppi, M. V. (1999). *International relations theory: Realism, pluralism, globalism, and beyond* (3rd edition). Pearson.

World Bank, Carbon Finance Unit. (2011). *BioCarbon Fund.* Retrieved from http://wbcarbonfinance.org/Router.cfm?Page=BioCF&FID=9708&ItemID=9708

World Bank, Carbon Finance Unit. (2015). *About the BioCarbon Fund.* Retrieved from https://wbcarbonfinance.org/Router.cfm?Page=BioCF&ft=About

6 Can REDD help developing countries achieve economic growth and mitigate climate change?

Introduction

Reducing Emissions from Deforestation and Forest Degradation (REDD) is receiving highest priority as one of the prominent means to mitigate emissions of global greenhouse gases (GHGs). REDD Plus goes beyond deforestation and forest degradation and includes the role of conservation, sustainable management of forests, and enhancement of forest carbon stocks. REDD is an attempt to create financial value for the carbon stored in forests, offering incentives for developing countries to reduce emissions from forested lands and invest in low-carbon paths to sustainable development. The proponents' central argument is that REDD funding contributes to sustainable management of forests for carbon storage to reduce global GHG emissions, poverty alleviation, and sustainable economic development and also contributes to biodiversity conservation in developing countries (see chapter 5).

But the questions of whether and how social co-benefits should be factored into REDD design and delivery are also widely debated. The first rationale is that the primary objective of REDD is to mitigate GHGs, not poverty. Poverty alleviation has been secondary and only added to the list later on. Therefore, the appropriate stance was to be that of "do no harm" to the poor. In contrast, the other rationale is that REDD would not succeed in developing countries and least developed countries unless a "pro-poor approach" for co-benefits are delivered. This group views REDD as deriving much of its legitimacy and potential effectiveness from its ability to improve the welfare of the forest-dependent poor and foster sustainable development in some of the poorest regions of the world. The arguments in favor of a pro-poor approach are varied and compelling. REDD could well prove high-risk for the forest-dependent poor and vulnerable population in each country that implements REDD projects. Some of the reasons include the multiplicity of interests and the polarization of the wealth and power of different stakeholders in the forest sector. Yet it can also be argued that

REDD can provide important opportunities to reduce poverty and enhance equity by delivering significant financial flows to rural areas, which are among the most depressed and underfunded parts of most developing and least developed economies.

However, there are some serious concerns that need attention before making a considered judgment on REDD's success. First, REDD is an initiative that is funded by developed countries, international organizations, and corporations in developing and least developed countries with the narrow view of receiving emissions quota as cash back for balancing their countries' domestic emissions ceilings. Second, success in REDD may result in unintended consequences such as the significant rise of an animal species to create imbalance in a biodiversity system owing to better conserved habitats and accidental forest fires due to accumulated fuel loads. Third, poor governance, non-inclusive decision-making processes, and political instability could lead to inequity in distribution of benefits, leading to further unsustainable exploitation of the forests. Fourth, there is concern about conflict in benefit sharing in the forestry sector, as there has been limited participation by the affected communities. Fifth, it is unclear whether the sustained interest of the donor community in the mitigation of GHGs through REDD funding will continue to exist for a long enough period of time. Sixth, it is unknown whether and how geographical, sectoral, and regional leakages of forests and forest products to meet the demands of the free market mechanism in the capitalist system would occur.

Previous researchers have contextualized few of the concerns raised above and have argued that if "good governance" is practiced, REDD would be able to achieve its objectives. However, as we have already shown in our previous chapters, a globalized capitalistic free market economy with its powerful influence of market mechanisms compels developing and least developed countries to provide raw materials to meet the demands of consumerist society and limits the success of REDD programs. In this chapter, we will address REDD's strengths and limitations. We ask: Can REDD help developing countries achieve economic growth and mitigate climate change? We contextualize the explanation of institutional constraints on REDD, which focuses on protection of the forests in the developing countries and least developed countries for carbon storage but does not help developed countries reduce emissions domestically. In addition, we argue that although REDD is being funded by developed countries, little has been done to decrease the demand for forest products and agricultural goods within the full-fledged function of global capitalism. Furthermore, we demonstrate that REDD increases the risk of perverse incentives toward monoculture forests, destroying the existing harmony in the biodiverse system. Finally, we address whether or not REDD will allow developing and least developed countries to achieve economic growth and alleviate poverty. We also analyze how each of the constraints noted above is part of REDD and why they will not allow REDD to achieve one of its important goals, that of reducing global GHG emissions to address the problems of climate change. We note that although it might help conserve the forests of some regions, REDD will alter the geography of forest use and promote unsustainable practices elsewhere.

Institutional constraints of REDD

The central rationale of REDD seems quite simple, easy, and accessible. The fundamental reasoning behind it is that developed countries are the parties responsible for creating the global warming problem to date. Therefore, they need to shoulder the burden of reducing GHGs to address climate change, and in doing so they need to pay the developing and least developed countries to keep their forests standing to reduce emissions from forest loss and degradation. However, this simplicity veils myriads of complex international and domestic laws, institutional constraints, tropical forest governance, and neoliberal market policies. Good forest governance is essential to any tropical rainforest country's government capacity to effectively formulate and implement REDD policies and legislation (Butt, Lyster, & Stephens, 2015). These include governance establishing baselines and national reference levels; Measurement, Reporting, and Verification; rights of tenure; rights of indigenous peoples and other forest-dependent communities; conservation of biodiversity; and the striking of a balance between the market economy and forest sustainability. Yet these governance issues have long been concerns for the international community, and little has been achieved so far (Butt, Lyster, & Stephens, 2015).

In chapter 4 we demonstrated that the underlying causes of deforestation vary from country to country and even within a country and are often complex in nature. While deforestation in Africa was mainly caused by conversion of forests for subsistence farming and commercial logging, in Latin America it resulted from conversion of forests for commercial agriculture and cattle farming, and in Asia there was a mixture of commercial logging and agriculture. The underlying causes are often even more intractable, ranging from governance structures, land tenure systems, and law enforcement issues, to the market economy and cultural value of forests, to the rights of indigenous people and local communities and benefit-sharing mechanisms, to poverty and food production policies. As a result, solutions to the problem cannot be generalized; they need to be specific to a locality and tailor-made to the environmental and socio-economic conditions of each country and its institutional capacity.

Although concerted efforts have been made by developing countries with the support of the international community for the past couple of decades or longer to reduce unplanned deforestation, stem forest degradation, and implement sustainable forest management, the challenges have proven to be considerable. The linkages between deforestation, development, and poverty are context-specific and complex. Weak governance and institutional capacity in some countries, as well as inadequate institutional mechanisms for effective participation by local communities in land-use decisions, could seriously compromise the delivery of both local and global benefits and the long-term sustainability of REDD investments. If REDD programs are not carefully designed and institutionalized, they could marginalize the landless and those with informal communal use-rights in the climate risk countries, compromising REDD's goals.

REDD governance is informed by two norms concerning who should take responsibility to mitigate GHG emissions and how to pursue the mitigation targets. These two norms stipulate that developed countries should take the lead in mitigating GHG emissions and that mitigation should be pursued via domestic targets and through funding to save forests elsewhere, in the developing or least developed countries. This means that developed countries, international organizations, and corporations are paying to keep the forests in the developing and least developed countries to obtain carbon credits for meeting their quantified targets domestically. However, some developed countries do not even have quantified targets yet. The United States is an example. The United States hasn't placed a real cap on GHG emissions, and it only recently recognized carbon dioxide as a contributing gas that should be regulated. Researchers have noted that developed countries are doing very little to reduce their actual domestic emissions (Pandey, 2014; International Energy Agency, 2010). REDD is undoubtedly a market mechanism. Developed countries have been the funders/buyers, and developing and least developed countries have been the receivers/sellers of carbon credits by protecting the forests in their jurisdiction. As explained in chapter 2, a variety of mechanisms, including programs of the United Nations and the World Bank, administer REDD funding. REDD finance is also considered in the international climate change negotiations and remains a key component of international climate change governance (Collins & Hicks, 2014). Under REDD, developed countries make payments for forest protection to developing countries, tied to performance in deforestation reduction, whereas the developed countries do very little to reduce emissions in their domestic territory.

While experts have attempted to demonstrate that REDD could significantly reduce GHG emissions and protect biodiversity, it is clearly not without its substantive problems. Questions arise about the fairness of the scheme, which focuses on reducing emissions caused by some of the world's poorest people while emissions are allowed to continue to rise rapidly in richer countries and among consumerist societies, which are the most prominent causes of global anthropogenic GHG emissions and climate change. Also, some developing countries are wary of foreign interference in their land-use and forest-use policies and have argued that environmentalism is a ploy of developed countries to halt development in the developing countries ever since the UN Conference on the Human Environment in Stockholm in 1972 has been sponsored (Watson & Pandey, 2015; World Commission on Environment and Development, 1987). Many researchers also highlight the operational concerns – such as the difficulty in monitoring and measuring deforestation rates, or attributing changes in deforestation to REDD finance (Pandey, 2015a). Many tropical forest countries do not possess the capabilities to address these challenges. The existing REDD institutions are bilateral, multilateral, and market-based mechanisms. Each of these institutions seems to have some potential, but they are also marred by various constraints on the long-term sustainability of the REDD or REDD Plus programs, as shown in chapter 5.

Is the demand for forest products falling?

Tropical forests are being cut down at an increasingly alarming rate without any significant counter-measures such as afforestation. This has created growing concerns over rapidly dwindling areas of tropical forests. This accelerated deforestation involves several socio-economic factors, which have been used to explain global tropical deforestation rates (Scrieciu, 2006). Global demand for wood products such as paper, furniture, and construction materials is a major cause of damage to tropical forests – and this demand has been projected to rapidly increase over the next half-century (Elias & Boucher, 2014). Forest product markets in developed countries have been steadily rising since 2010 after two years of stagnancy in production and consumption. According to the United Nations Economic Commission for Europe (UNECE, 2011, p. 1), "Consumption of forest products in the UNECE region rose by 5.6% overall in 2010, with small differences between the three subregions: consumption rose by 4.1% in North America, by 6.6% in Europe and 6.3% in the Commonwealth of Independent States." The wood energy sector is continually growing as public policies and financial incentives have pushed the expansion of modern technology for generating heat, heat and electricity, or electricity alone. Germany's decision to shut down all its nuclear energy plants by 2022 is accelerating coal and oil price increases, and the impact of the nuclear disaster in Fukushima, Japan, has made governments around the world reconsider their policies on nuclear energy, helping to drive up the demand for wood energy (UNECE, 2011).

The demand for forest products is rising not only in developed countries but also among the "pockets of rich" in emerging economies such as India and China. In response to this rising demand for forest products globally, China has been the largest producer of wood-based panels, paper, pulp, and paperboard. Its products also include textiles and food additives based on cellulose, optical screens for laptops, casings for televisions, computers, mobile telephones, computer keyboards, and even furniture. Although the expansion of Chinese forests has occurred in that country, China has been developing an immense export industry for wood and paper products. "China is now the 'wood workshop for the world,' according to Forest Trends, a Washington, D.C.-based think tank, consuming more than 400 million cubic meters of timber annually to feed both its burgeoning exports and growing domestic demands" (Laurance, 2011, p. 1). In its fervor to secure timber, China is increasingly seen as a predator on the world's forests, from Southeast Asia, to Latin America, to sub-Saharan Africa. The pulp, paper, and other products derived from forests and used by Chinese manufacturers to make branded products are used by scores of well-known companies in the developed countries around the world. Some of these companies include Gucci, Scholastic, Hachette, Tiffany & Co., Prada, American Greetings, Marc Jacobs, and the Rupert Murdoch–owned HarperCollins publishing – which are continuously using forest products supplied by Chinese manufacturers (Laurance, 2011).

The increasing unsustainable global demand for forest products has serious implications for our global economic system, in addition to its consequences for REDD and sustainable forest management. To meet the rising demand for forest supplies, forests are being cut down rapidly, and as one region of forest is consumed, the corporations keep moving on to other regions. For example, to meet the global demand for forest products and commercial agriculture, large portions of Indonesian forests have been deforested. The Norwegian government signed a deal with Indonesia to stop deforestation to restore deforested areas. This is a good beginning, but the most serious question is: did we stop consuming forest products? If not, the companies are likely to go to Malaysia or sub-Saharan Africa or elsewhere now, instead of Indonesia, to get forest resources for their productions to meet the demand of consumerist societies and countries around the world. This means that unless we fix the leakage and global economy of the high-consuming world, REDD will achieve very little in terms of GHG mitigation and forest conservation, but rather will continue global deforestation in an illusive way. The unsustainable exploitation of forest resources for exports from peripheral countries will continue to exist, as argued in theories of world systems and dependency (see Wallerstein, 1974).

The economic interests of developing countries also play a critical role in deforestation for the production of soybeans, beef, cattle, palm oil, and timber and pulp, as well as for fuelwood and subsistence farming. In chapter 4, we demonstrated that the direct drivers of deforestation vary a great deal between continents and regions, yet the indirect drivers in all regions can be narrowed down to subsistence farming and economic/commercial interests. It was also noted that, apart from subsistence farming, other drivers of deforestation are driven purely by the economic interests of the developing or least developed countries, either to service their foreign loans or to continue their agenda of domestic economic growth and development. The debt crises highlight the inability of many poor nations to generate enough revenue to service their foreign debt. Initial evidence that deforestation and indebtedness are interlinked came from correlations between countries' debt and deforestation in those countries (Ayres, 1989). According to the World Resources Institute (1992, p. 12):

> Debt payments often constitute a large share of the national budget, squeezing out needed investments in environmental protection or economic and human development. In some countries, debt service obligations are so large that they exceed new loans and private external investment, meaning that financial resources are flowing out of, rather than into, the country.

Kahn and McDonald's (1995) research outputs also indicated that debt is an important factor in deforestation in tropical countries. In the 1970s and 1980s, many developing and least developing countries over-borrowed from international financial institutions relative to their ability to pay the debt back. According to the World Bank's *World Development Report 1992*, Bolivia, Brazil, Democratic Republic of Congo, and Peru, among others, were the countries that over-borrowed and suffered in terms of repayment (World Bank, 1992). Their inability to repay and continuous accumulation of debt have often interfered with the development processes of the borrowing countries. Although many factors may affect the level of deforestation and generate a disparity between the actual and optimal level of deforestation, the payment of debt has been the most dominant. Kahn and McDonald (1995, p. 122) argued:

> Our study develops a behavioural model, which suggests that debt can lead to myopic behaviour, leading to deforestation rates that may not be optimal in the long run, but are necessary in the short run to meet current constraints. The constrained optimizing equations for deforestation, which were derived from the models, were estimated using

two-stage least-squares regressions, which showed that the relationship between deforestation and debt was statistically strong.

The International Monetary Fund (IMF) and World Bank have responded to the debt crisis by providing structural adjustment loans that are assumed to resolve the balance-of-payment issues. There are a variety of options available to a country to deal with its debt problem, such as debt rescheduling, debt repudiation, increased borrowing, devaluation of the domestic currency, restriction of imports, and increases in exports. Debt rescheduling refers to an agreed delay in the repayment of a debt, usually applying to both interest and principal payments, and also often involving a renegotiation of the terms. Debt repudiation refers to the refusal of public authorities to acknowledge or pay a debt because of their fragile financial circumstances. Increased borrowing allows the countries to repay the previous loans but puts them in danger of paying more in the coming years; it provides them time to make their economy vibrant so that they could be able to pay the next debt when it matures. Countries can also devaluate their currency to continue their export-driven economies; however, this usually does not help developing countries, who most often export cheap raw materials and import more expensive goods. The other option for dealing with the debt is reducing imports and increasing exports, which will help boost the economy. Although the options noted above are available for dealing with debt service, the structural adjustment programs of international financial institutions require governments to promote economic activity with comparative advantages, and this often involves exports of whatever natural resources are in demand on the world market (Peet, 2003; McMichael, 2003). The sectors that cause deforestation either to achieve national economic interests or to service debts include logging, ranching, mining, and agriculture, and most of these exports are destined for the rich nations of the world (Peet, 2003; McMichael, 2003).

Peru's forested area is the second largest in Latin America and the ninth largest in the world. Yet Peruvian forests and their peoples, rich in biological and cultural diversity, are nonetheless in a state of constant risk. The country's macroeconomic "growth" has come hand in hand with various activities that are destructive to the Amazon rainforest and the people who live there. Despite the fact that 84 percent of the Amazon region is under concession for oil and gas industry activity, it is small farmers who are being singled out as the main drivers of deforestation. This situation has placed the Peruvian Amazon in the sights of numerous multilateral and private finance mechanisms, non-governmental organizations (NGOs), brokers, and consultants who are seeking to expand their businesses and profits with the help of the REDD Plus mechanism (Cabello, 2014). Also, deforestation for debt service was clearly found in many other developing countries, including Bolivia, Brazil, and Indonesia.

In the 1980s Bolivia faced an extraordinary economic crisis. Bolivia suffered from major external shocks, but the extent of economic collapse in the face of these shocks, including hyperinflation during 1984 and 1985, suggests that internal factors as well as external shocks have been critical to Bolivia's poor economic performance (Morales & Sachs, 1988). Bolivia is one of the poorest countries in the Western Hemisphere and is dependent on foreign governments and foreign aid from multilateral lenders (Morales & Sachs, 1988). In 1984 Bolivia became the first Latin American country to declare an official moratorium on debt payments to commercial banks, and it continued to withhold payment through 1988 (Hudson & Hanratty, 1989). Bolivia was not able to pay its high international debt until it adopted extractive industries for an export-driven economy. Bolivian forests were also affected by the crisis. In 1987 Conservation International initiated the first "debt-for-nature swap" when it purchased US$650,000 worth of Bolivian debt for only US$100,000 (Hudson & Hanratty, 1989). In exchange for being relieved of the obligation to repay a portion of its international debt, the country agreed to set aside funds to promote conservation by encouraging sustainable development, expanding environmental education programs, purchasing land, and improving land management.

The debt crisis of the 1980s was the most serious case in Brazil. Brazil's economic growth and income stagnated because of the need to reduce imports. Unemployment rose to high levels, and inflation reduced the buying power of the middle classes. Before the economic crisis, Brazil had borrowed money to enhance its economic stability and reduce the poverty rate. However, as Brazil was unable to pay back its foreign debts, loans ceased, stopping the flow of resources previously available for the innovations and improvements of the previous few years. Brazil had to borrow money from the International Monetary Fund and practice structural adjustment programs as directed by the fund. In parallel, Brazil also had the highest rate of deforestation in the 1980s. For servicing foreign debt during Brazil's economic crisis, large development projects have occurred, leading to large-scale deforestation (Hanley, Shorgren, & White, 2013).

In 1997–1998 Southeast Asian countries, including Indonesia, faced an economic crisis caused largely by speculation and capital flight, leading to a sharp fall in currency values, followed by a great depression (Humphreys, 2006). Indonesia had to borrow from the IMF on the condition that Indonesia would practice austerity and structural adjustment policies. The IMF's letter of intent clearly recommended that the Indonesian government remove all formal and informal restrictions on investment in palm oil plantations (Humphreys, 2006). This led to increased forest fires for commercial plantations of oil palm. One of the worst outcomes of the IMF recommendations was an increased and accelerated rate of deforestation.

Kahn and McDonald (1995) argued that deforestation could be either a direct or indirect cause of debt servicing. The concept of "debt-for-nature swaps" was also introduced to assist with debt servicing and halt the massive deforestation. The concept of "debt-for-nature swaps" is a major source of international nature conservation funding, and the swaps have been publicized as a win–win solution to the problem of how to finance conservation in the developing world (Fuller, 1989). The United States signed an agreement to forgive nearly US$30 million in Indonesian debt in return for protecting the forests on Sumatra Island, which is home to endangered tigers, elephants, rhinos, and orangutans (Wright, 2009). Recognizing that Indonesia has one of the highest deforestation rates in the world and was losing an area of forest the size of Switzerland annually, the Norwegian government also signed a US$1 billion deal with the Indonesian government aimed at reducing deforestation (Lang, 2010).

Tropical deforestation has become an issue of global environmental concern, due to its substantial negative repercussions for the global climate and biodiversity, fostered by the failure of capitalistic economic systems to reflect the true value of the environment (Scrieciu, 2006). Global tropical forests are encountering a grim future unless humans adopt a radically different approach to protecting and managing them, warns a review recently published in the journal *Science* (Lewis, Edwards, & Galbraith, 2015). It argues that the path begins with selective logging, which opens up intact forest landscapes to hunters and additional impacts, and finishes with a stripped or converted landscape. These trends and changes raise serious concerns about the state of tropical forests toward the end of the century (Lewis, Edwards, & Galbraith, 2015).

Monoculture forests to gain perverse incentive by decreasing biodiversity

At the sixth session of the United Nations Forum on Forests (UNFF) in 2006, delegates of UN member states decided to set shared global objectives related to forests and agreed to work globally and nationally to achieve progress toward the protection of forests and sustainable forest management. The meeting identified four objectives (UNFF, 2015). The first is to reverse forest loss. This objective aims to reverse the loss of forest cover worldwide through sustainable forest management, including protection, restoration, afforestation, and reforestation, and to increase efforts to prevent forest degradation. The second objective is to enhance forest-based benefits, which means economic, social, and environmental benefits, which includes improving the livelihoods of forest-dependent people. The third objective is to increase sustainably managed forest areas, comprising protected forests, and to increase the proportion of forest products derived from sustainably managed forests. The fourth objective is to mobilize financial resources to reverse the decline in official development assistance for sustainable forest management and to mobilize significantly increased new and additional financial resources from all sources for the implementation of sustainable forest management. The UNFF encourages member states to effectively implement sustainable forest management practices to address emerging forest-related challenges such as climate change, loss of forest cover, forest degradation, desertification, and biodiversity loss. The United Nations Collaborative Programme on Reducing Emissions from Deforestation and Forest Degradation in Developing Countries (UN-REDD Programme) works closely with the Secretariat of the United Nations Framework Convention on Climate Change and the Global Environment Facility, as well as the UNFF, members of the Collaborative Partnership on Forests, donors, civil society, non-governmental organizations, and academia to achieve these goals, as mentioned earlier.

Other key collaborating partners of the UN-REDD Programme include the Forest Carbon Partnership Facility (FCPF) and the Forest Investment Program, for the elaboration of existing commitments to coordinate and work within strategic partnerships. For example, in the context of piloting multiple delivery partners for the FCPF Readiness Fund, the World Bank and the UN-REDD Programme agencies are developing common social and environmental principles (UN-REDD Programme, 2011). However, the UN-REDD documents (2011) have identified four issues that are of some concern: (1) REDD will lock up forests by decoupling conservation from development; (2) asymmetric power distribution will enable powerful REDD consortia to deprive communities of their legitimate land-development aspirations; (3) hard-fought gains in forest management practices will be wasted; and (4) commercial REDD may erode culturally rooted not-for-profit conservation values. We describe the four issues in brief below:

The first concern is that REDD will lock up forests by decoupling conservation from development. REDD is primarily focused on treating forests as carbon sinks to reduce global GHGs and then on alleviating poverty, leading to sustainable economic development. As it gives the maximum priority to conserving the forest, people dependent on forests may be deprived of forest resources because of REDD's strong focus on forest protection, thereby taking them off the path toward sustainable forest management and local development. The second concern is about asymmetric power distribution, which will enable powerful REDD consortia to deprive communities of their legitimate land-development aspirations. This issue is interconnected with the first one. Although environmental decision-making processes are expected to be participatory, they are often driven by elites. The poor and vulnerable may participate, but they usually seem to have little voice in the final steps of decision making. The third is that hard-fought gains in forest management practices will be wasted. Community forest management practices have long existed. For example, Nepal has one of the best community forest management practices in the history of community forest management. The forest resources are managed appropriately by members of the community, and they have been used in a very sustainable way for the long time. The communities do not consider forest only as the provider of the resources; rather, the intrinsic value of the forest is also emphasized for its sustainability. Ostrom's book *Governing the Commons* (1992) offers excellent examples of how locals have managed their local resources in a very sustainable way. However, REDD focuses on conservation and payment of the certified units more than on sustainable use of the forests by the community, as noted earlier, which means that commercial REDD may erode culturally rooted not-for-profit conservation values and may also contribute to eroding the hard-fought practices of community forest management.

The interactions between expanded human activities and environmental systems have been causing forest changes as well as environmental degradation. Farmers and land managers constantly make trade-offs between different land-use opportunities and the constraints imposed by a variety of external factors. The direct and indirect causes of deforestation and forest degradation are the actual drivers of forest change. These drivers may differ among regions and countries, and may often exist outside the forest sector, such as interest in economic gains, development, and the global economic system. The sustainability and viability of REDD Plus depend on changing business-as-usual activities in sectors currently driving GHG emissions from deforestation and forest degradation. One of the most prominent causes of deforestation is anthropogenic activities that impact the forest cover and result in loss of carbon stocks. Agriculture is estimated to be the largest direct driver, accounting for about 80 percent of deforestation worldwide (Kissinger, Herold, & De Sy, 2012). Mining, infrastructure, and urban expansion are important but less prominent (Kissinger, Herold, & De Sy, 2012). Major drivers of forest degradation include unsustainable logging (both legal and illegal) and the use of fuelwood and charcoal, the latter in particular in sub-Saharan Africa. Indirect drivers for both deforestation and forest degradation include a range of forces combining social, economic, political, technological, and cultural factors that operate at a range of scales and are often interrelated.

The other prominent factors in altering the forest cover are international economic interests in an ecosystem's sustainability. Except for "lip service," businesses do not intend to strike a balance between economics and environmental sustainability. Examples include tropical deforestation for economic gains in Indonesia, Vietnam, Brazil, and many other countries. First, the natural forests are exploited for economic incentives by destroying the harmony of the ecosystem and its biodiversity. Then, a tree plantation is considered to be the solution to revert back to natural forests and mitigate climate change. Symmetrical tree plantations are considered to be the panacea. In a monoculture (the agricultural practice of growing a single crop or plant species in a field at a time), trees are planted for the sake of keeping the forests green, but at the same time forests at another location are destroyed to continue supporting the economic interests of the relevant stakeholders, agents, and global economic systems. The most discernible obstruction is that most tree plantations are timber crops, planned to be cut down for pulp, timber, or saw-wood within a relatively short time (Mutter & Overbeek, 2011). They are also prone to fire, and their monoculture, even-aged, single-species composition makes them vulnerable to high levels of damage through disease, wind, and drought. Several researchers have demonstrated that when an ecosystem is destroyed for a monoculture plantation, biodiversity suffers (Carbon Trade Watch, 2015). For example, a study of lizards and frogs in the Amazon showed that primary forests contained far more species, whereas industrial plantations allowed the survival of only a few habitat-generalists. Therefore, monoculture tree plantations neither contribute in the long term to a meaningful reduction in the global carbon emissions that cause climate change nor sustain the ecosystems but only contribute, at best, to temporary reductions in carbon emissions (Carbon Trade Watch, 2015).

In 2010, field studies conducted by researchers from Timberwatch and Envirocare revealed significant direct and indirect negative impacts on the livelihoods of communities in Idete, Tanzania, such as displacement; poor working conditions; the destruction of biodiversity on which communities rely for food, fuel, and medicines; and reduced water availability. The overall objective of this monoculture plantation is to contribute to meeting the growing demand for quality wood products and economic gains. The species planted are mainly pines and eucalyptus, and they can be invasive (Forest Carbon Portal, 2003). In Asia-Pacific, especially in Malaysia, Indonesia, and Papua New Guinea, demand for palm oil has resulted in large-scale conversion of tropical forests. In Africa rubber, wood pulp, and cacao, in addition to palm oil, are the commercial products. Moreover, monoculture tree plantations have affected most countries in Asia-Pacific, Latin America, and Africa. For example, in Brazil, Argentina, Chile, Ecuador, and Uruguay, pine and eucalyptus are grown for timber and other export products. In Colombia and Venezuela, palm is also grown for biofuels. Malaysia has recently stated that it intends to expand palm oil production into the Amazon (Hance, 2008). Sandy Gauntlett of the Pacific Indigenous Peoples Environment Coalition shared his experience, noting, "Tree plantations are not forests. A plantation is a highly uniform agricultural system that replaces natural ecosystems and their rich biodiversity. The trees planted are geared to the production of a single raw material, whether it is timber, pulp, rubber, palm oil or others" (quoted in Hance, 2008). Displaying solidarity against monoculture tree plantations, "a number of environmental and social organizations have declared September 21st International Day against Monoculture Tree Plantations to highlight the social upheaval and environmental degradation including impacts on global biodiversity and climate change wrought by industrial plantations" (Hance, 2008).

Yet the European Parliament is promoting the second generation of biofuels produced from wood. Likewise, forestry firms in the United States are pushing the US government to do the same. Government agencies in countries like New Zealand and international organizations like the Food and Agriculture Organization and the World Bank incorrectly define plantations as forests, despite abundant documentation that proves that the only thing they have in common is that the trees are present in the forests to be used as exports for profits. Gauntlett argues, "By calling them [monoculture plantations] forests, these institutions and governments help to impose and perpetuate an unsustainable monoculture plantation production model" (Carbon Trade Watch, 2008). Simone Lovera of the Global Forest Coalition emphasizes, "Plantations form part of an industrial model for the production of abundant and cheap raw material that serves as an input for the economic growth of the industrialized countries. What the producer countries get are environmental degradation and rising poverty, which are the 'externalized costs' of this cheap raw material" (Carbon Trade Watch, 2008).

Governments, along with industries from major emitting countries, have remained unwilling to take action against climate change because there are no simple solutions, unlike with ozone depletion and the Montreal Protocol (Depledge & Yamin, 2009; Paterson & Grubb, 1992; Pandey, 2014). Climate change policy requires limiting the use of fossil fuels, which have been the economic lifeblood of industrialized and industrializing societies. "The structural causes for climate change are linked to the current capitalist hegemonic system. Fighting the climate change involves changing the system" (Margarita Declaration, 2014). As long as the green economy does not imply restructuring present patterns of production, consumption, service provision, and finance, it will allow an increase in industrial tree plantations, resulting in less biodiversity and reduced livelihood opportunities for forest peoples by destroying natural forests. It will also enable forests to be traded as mere carbon sinks and reservoirs, alienated from their social, cultural, spiritual, and nurturing roles. The superfluous green economy will only help to maintain and even reinforce the polluting patterns that are at the root of the present global change and climate crisis.

"Countries largely define strategies and interventions to deal with national and local scale drivers, but face problems addressing international drivers and acknowledge that international pressure will increase" (Margarita Declaration, 2014). Despite earlier promises, most governments have failed to reduce GHG emissions, aside from some easy wins: for example, in the United Kingdom, the switch from more polluting oil and coal to slightly less polluting gas. Reductions were often counteracted by other increases and the mantras of cornucopian economic growth (Pandey, 2015b). To arrest climate change is to adopt a transformative policy stance for a different economic system rather than adopting the paths of monoculture tree plantations within the framework of REDD or REDD Plus and business-as-usual economic systems. Large-scale monoculture tree plantations cause serious environmental, social, and economic impacts on local communities. These impacts have been amply documented around the world and include the depletion of water sources owing to changes in the hydrological cycle; deterioration of rivers and streams; air and water pollution resulting from the use of pesticides and other agrochemicals; the displacement of entire communities when their land is occupied by plantations; violations of human, labor, and environmental rights; differentiated impacts on women; the deterioration of cultural diversity; widespread violence; and the critical loss of biodiversity (Carbon Trade Watch, 2008).

REDD and economic growth in developing or least developed countries

Although emissions reductions are the central goal of REDD, poverty alleviation and the economic development of the participating countries are given equal salience. Like other payment for ecosystem services (PES) schemes, these objectives are coupled with the goal of sustainable development in the participating REDD countries. As already pointed out, one of the greatest barriers to sustainable development is the inequitable way in which carbon markets distribute benefits within the current economic system. As McAfee (2012, p. 108) describes, the current economic system uses the market to determine "uses of productive resources and the distribution of what is produced." Considering that the invisible hand of the market pursues development, the neoliberal economic policy was introduced to bring development to the developing and least developed countries through globalization and economic growth by removing barriers to capital flow (McAfee, 2012, p. 108). This economic growth was meant to mitigate environmental problems and address the concerns of poverty in developing and least developed countries through sustainable economic growth. This leads to the linking of environmental improvement with sustainable development under "liberal environmentalism." This ideology contributed to the creation of the Clean Development Mechanism (CDM) as a part of the Kyoto Protocol with goals of "economic development and climate mitigation" (Bohr & Dill, 2011, p. 414). It is hard to imagine PES schemes, such as the CDM and REDD, achieving sustainable development when neoliberal economics and globalization have failed to bring about poverty reduction (McAfee, 2012, p. 108) because PES schemes rely on "the market" to achieve conservation but there are barriers that stand in the way of the economic growth in the poorest of countries. Carbon markets rely on the investment of actors, public or private, to create projects that lead to certified emission reductions. The planning process for these projects can be incredibly costly, with CDM project planning costing between US$40,000 to US$600,000 (United Nations Environment Programme, 2007, p. 55). Not only is the creation of a project costly, but each participating country is associated with varying amounts of risk, such as poor infrastructure or the possibility of war, that may affect the future profitability of certified emission reductions. A perfect example of a high-risk region is sub-Saharan Africa, which has poor infrastructure and institutional capacity, a lack of skilled labor, and isolated rural communities (Timilsina et al., 2010, p. 94). Investors in the carbon market, much like any market, seek the greatest profitability and minimum risk. It just so happens that possible sites showing the greatest amount of risk are found in the poor, isolated communities most in need of developmental assistance. Because of this barrier, CDM projects in least developed countries, like those in sub-Saharan Africa, account for 2.6 percent of the total market, whereas the largest number of CDM projects are located in developing countries such as China, India, and South Africa (Bohr & Dill, 2011, p. 420). Of the 20 CDM projects established in sub-Saharan Africa, 15 can be found in South Africa (Timilsina et al., 2010, p. 94), a country with much stronger infrastructure and institutional capacity. This is extremely relevant to REDD, as the implementation of REDD projects is extremely costly and requires a long-term commitment from investors (Streck, 2013, p. 125).

Sustainable development of small forest communities cannot be achieved while simultaneously focusing on market efficiency. REDD, like other PES schemes, requires that actors compensate participants at or above their opportunity costs. As it relates to REDD, opportunity cost is the "forgone revenue from alternative land uses" (Streck, 2013, p. 108). Much like risk, opportunity costs vary significantly depending on project location. Opportunity costs may be much higher for large, prosperous landowners who are much more capable of conducting large-scale deforestation than are small groups of land-based indigenous groups (McAfee, 2012, p. 121). Opportunity costs are established by developed countries investing in REDD; setting them is no simple task and requires political decision making (Lohmann, 2009, p. 169). The result of unequal opportunity costs would be large-scale payments in areas of active deforestation while indigenous groups who live in areas where forests are preserved year in and year out receive nothing (Rudel, 2013). Also, the phenomenon known as diseconomies of scale, where average costs increase as output increases, has an inequitable effect in a PES scheme. This phenomenon results in much higher transaction costs when dealing with many small holders as opposed to a few large, prosperous landholders (McAfee, 2012, p. 117). Therefore, markets will drive investment away from the many poor, rural communities who are intended to receive the developmental benefits of REDD and other PES schemes.

There are even more barriers as a result of REDD that could prevent real economic growth in developing countries. As mentioned above, it is important to note that REDD began purely with goals of emissions reductions from avoided deforestation that could eventually be traded in a carbon market. It was only after much intervention from local and international NGOs such as Indonesian Friends of Earth and the Indigenous Peoples Alliance of the Archipelago, that a shift occurred toward the "conservation-as-development" project that it has become today (Howell, 2014, p. 257). The results of this shift can be observed in the varying levels of safeguarding undertaken by the different organizations for operationalizing REDD. These safeguards are added to REDD policies to prevent any undue harm caused by REDD or the organizations involved. An example of a safeguard employed by the UN-REDD Programme is the requirement of free, prior, and informed consent by indigenous groups or other forest-dependent communities before beginning to implement REDD policy (McDermott et al., 2012). Despite efforts by operationalizing organizations to minimize the social risks of implementing REDD, there is no official agreement over safeguarding requirements to receive a future performance-based payment. This ambiguity embedded within the policy makes it a "boundary object." McDermott et al. (2012, p. 64) defines this boundary object as a policy that is "plastic, open to interpretation by different actors and valuable to each for different reasons." As Howell (2014) mentions, despite efforts to improve safeguards and transparency in participating countries, the uncertainties embedded within the policy prevent effective and safe development. These uncertainties include whether, how much, and when communities will be paid, as well as what the source and form of the payments will be. Even if free, prior, and informed consent is required, or consultation in the case of the FCPF (McDermott et al., 2012), it is clear that forest communities cannot make an informed decision given the ambiguity in the policy.

Even with safeguards being established, it is difficult to say whether developmental benefits will be received at the local level. There is great ambiguity over not only how much REDD participants will receive but exactly how it will be received. Because of high transaction costs and/or poor valuation of opportunity costs, participants may receive only the benefits of secure land tenure or improved environmental quality (Peskett, 2013). As Peskett (2013) describes, in order to minimize risk, the clear benefits and costs of REDD projects need to be provided to participants. In Howell's (2014) studies of Indonesia, this has not been the case. Even with increased involvement from local and foreign activists, villagers express great dissatisfaction with the operationalizing organization's lack of transparency and cooperation. This is not necessarily the fault of NGOs, as knowledge sharing can be difficult. This is certainly the case in Tanzania's Angai Forest, where villages are spread thinly and require coordination that is very difficult to attain (Mustalahti et al., 2012). This area of land in Tanzania has previously participated in a forest preservation project similar to REDD where villagers are meant to receive financial benefits for preserving forest stocks. The results of the project are not promising for future REDD successes, as, despite its conception in the late 1990s, villagers' land-management plans still have not been approved nearly 15 years later (Mustalahti et al., 2012). This lack of transparency has been seen in cases where projects occur in areas where indigenous groups secure land tenure. This is not always the case, as in many developing countries over half of the land is considered state land (Neilson & Leimona, 2013).

Despite the fact that many indigenous groups have rights of access on state lands, land grabbing could be a possibility as a result of higher land values under a REDD mechanism if governments decide to exercise their rights as owners of the land. This is entirely possible, if one takes the land-tenure rights of indigenous groups of Brazil as an example. These groups have the right to exploit the resources of occupied land such as soil, rivers, and lakes, but the federal government has the capacity to exploit the water and mineral resources of these lands in certain cases (Butt et al., 2013). This has resulted in the incorporation of the establishment of clear land-tenure rights into the requirements of projects (Neilson & Leimona, 2013). As Lemaitre shows in Guyana, a lack of progress on establishing land tenure has not stopped the FCPF from approving its readiness plans despite explicitly naming it an objective of the process. A study done by FERN and the Forest Peoples Programme critically reviewed the FCPF and the readiness preparation proposals (R-PPs) they helped to create and found that its policies and guidelines to minimize social risks are mere "lip service." Consultation and the ability to consider forest peoples' ideas have been inadequate. Most alarming, "R-PPs reaffirm state ownership over forestlands and most focus on valuation and monitoring of forest carbon to the exclusion of livelihood, biodiversity and cultural values" (Dooley et al., 2011, p. 7). These results support Howell's (2014) observations of UN-REDD and NGOs in Indonesia that indicate poor transparency and minimal progress in establishing land-tenure rights. Even in areas where community land tenure is secure, there is still ambiguity over the rights to the carbon stored in the trees found on community land. Because of the high transaction costs associated with project implementation, REDD is largely project based with private investors helping participating landowners cover these costs. Since investors fund the implementation, they could then be entitled to claim the rights to the carbon credits and therefore the carbon trading revenues if these rights are not explicitly made clear. Projects have proceeded without clarity over who has carbon rights, leaving no certainty over how future revenues will be distributed (Butt et al., 2013).

Because REDD projects are moving so quickly, not only have there been questions of land-tenure rights, but the legal frameworks of participating countries have prevented effective developmental gains in forest communities. A perfect example of this is the Indonesian government, which has seen a rapid decentralization of power following the fall of the Suharto's regime in 1998 (Butt et al., 2013). The result of this has been large-scale corruption and a failure to protect the rights of rural communities (Butt et al., 2013). An example of this corruption can be found in a previous policy known as the Reforestation Fund. In many cases, funds from this program were lost in the government and never contributed to reforestation projects. Also common was creation of fake projects as avenues for funds (Barr et al., 2010). And, as Howell (2014, p. 260) points out, the highly corrupt nature of the Ministry of Forestry is an "open secret." As a result of efforts by NGOs seeking to protect the rights of forest residents in a situation of much corruption and political failure, a moratorium on new REDD permitting has been declared (Butt et al., 2013). Despite this moratorium, Indonesia's rate of deforestation continues to rise and is now the world's highest (Butler, 2014). This can be attributed to, unsurprisingly, unclear policy on which areas are protected by the moratorium. Threats of corruption can be found outside of Indonesia, even in democratic countries like Brazil with stronger political institutions (Butt et al., 2013). These threats of corruption arise from the opportunity that REDD provides with its national policy-making process of establishing readiness that could possibly be influenced by powerful commercial interests, thus making corruption viable beyond the readiness phase (Dermawan et al., 2011). In addition, the incentive for corruption associated with illegal logging is expected to increase in the future, as timber prices are likely to increase with demand remaining high. Another example of the corruption that may arise under REDD can be found in Papua New Guinea, where, because the country lacks any regulatory framework, the government issued numerous carbon credits to companies that hadn't actually invested in any REDD assets (Lang, 2009).

Conclusion

This chapter has explored the research question of whether REDD can and will be able to assist developing and least developed countries to achieve sustainable economic growth, to alleviate poverty, and to mitigate global emissions. We approached this question from four different perspectives. The first approach we have adopted was REDD and its institutional constraints. The existing REDD institutions are bilateral, multilateral, and market-based mechanisms. Each of these institutions does seem to have some potential, but they are also marred by various constraints on the long-term sustainability of the REDD or REDD Plus programs. The operational concerns – such as the difficulty in monitoring and measuring deforestation rates, or in attributing changes in deforestation to REDD finance – are only some of the limitations of REDD institutions. The second approach we have taken was to consider whether the demand for forest products is falling. The data used in the analysis vividly demonstrated that the demand for forest products is not falling but rather is steadily increasing in the developed countries as well as in the "pockets of rich" in developing countries. The implication is that implementing REDD in one place with a focus on conservation to develop the forests as carbon sinks means shifting the geography of where forest products are obtained, owing to leakage in this modern economic system.

The third approach we have adopted was to examine afforestation, especially focusing on monoculture tree plantations for recovery of the forests. The research showed that reforestation is important but that monoculture tree plantations are mainly focused on economic gains. They are not actually forests but rather are cash crops to earn profits – supported by perverse incentives to decrease the harmony of biodiversity. The fourth approach we have adopted was to explore whether REDD could help achieve economic growth. We found that REDD investors were more interested in profits from implementing projects than in issues of local economic development and sustainable forest management. Thus, we argued that REDD would do very little in terms of sustainable economic development, poverty alleviation, and mitigation of GHGs in developing and least developed countries except that it provides benefits to investors, local elites, and power centers.

References

Ayres, J. M. (1989). Debt-for-equity swaps and the conservation of tropical rain forests. *Trends in Ecology and Evolution, 4*, 331–332.

Barr, C., Dermawan, A., Purnomo, H., & Komarudin, H. (2010). *Financial governance and Indonesia's Reforestation Fund during the Soeharto and post-Soeharto periods, 1989–2009.* Occasional Paper 52. Center for International Forestry. Retrieved from https://cgspace.cgiar.org/handle/10568/20265

Bohr, J., & Dill, B. (2011). Who benefits from market-based carbon mitigation. *Perspectives on Global Development and Technology, 10*, 406–428.

Butler, R. A. (2014, June). Despite moratorium, Indonesia now has the world's highest deforestation rate. *Mongabay.* Retrieved from http://www.mongabay.com

Butt, S., Garcia, B., Parsons, J., & Stephens, T. (2013). Brazil and Indonesia: REaDD+y or not? In R. Lyster, C. Mackenzie, & C. McDermott (Eds.), *Law, tropical forests, and carbon*, 251–274. Cambridge, UK: Cambridge University Press.

Butt, S., Lyster, R., & Stephens, T. (2015). *Climate change and forest governance: Lessons from Indonesia.* London: Routledge.

Cabello, J. (2014). Masking the destruction: REDD+ in the Peruvian Amazon. *Carbon Trade Watch.* Retrieved from http://www.carbontradewatch.org/articles/masking-the-destruction-redd-in-the-peruvian-amazon.html

Carbon Trade Watch. (2008). *Joint Release from World Rainforest Movement, Friends of the Earth International and Global Forest Coalition—groups call for action on 21 September: International Day against Monoculture Tree Plantations.* Retrieved from http://www.carbontradewatch.org/index.php?option=com_content&task=view&id=212&Itemid=36

Carbon Trade Watch. (2015). *Monocultures.* Retrieved from http://www.carbontradewatch.org/issues/monoculture.html

Collins, M., & Hicks, N. (2014, Dec. 19). What's REDD and will it help tackle climate change? *The Guardian.* Retrieved from http://www.theguardian.com/environment/2012/dec/19/what-is-redd-climate-change-deforestation

Depledge, J., & Yamin, F. (2009). The global climate change regime: A defense. In D. Helm & C. Hepburn (Eds.), *The economics and politics of climate change*, 433–453. New York, NY: Oxford University Press.

Dermawan, A., Petkova, E., Sinaga, A., Muhajir, M., & Indriatmoko, Y. (2011). *Preventing the risk of corruption in REDD+ in Indonesia.* Working Paper 80. Center for International Forestry Research. Retrieved from http://www.cifor.org/library/3476/preventing-the-risks-of-corruption-in-redd-in-indonesia/

Dooley, K., Griffiths, T., Martone, F., & Ozinga, S. (2011). Smoke and mirrors: A critical assessment of the Forest Carbon Partnership Facility. FERN and Forest Peoples Programme. Retrieved from http://www.forestpeoples.org/sites/fpp/files/publication/2011/03/smokeandmirrorsinternet.pdf

Elias, P., & Boucher, D. (2014). *Planting for the future: How demand for wood products could be friendly to tropical forests.* Cambridge, MA: Union of Concerned Scientists. Retrieved from http://www.ucsusa.org/sites/default/files/attach/2014/10/planting-for-the-future.pdf

Forest Carbon Portal. (2003). *Reforestation at the Idete Forest Project in the Southern Highlands of Tanzania.* Retrieved from http://www.forestcarbonportal.com/project/reforestation-idete-forest-project-southern-highlands-tanzania

Fuller, K. S. (1989). Debt-for-nature-swaps. *Environmental Science & Technology, 23*(12), 1450–1451.

Hance, J. (2008, Sept.). Monoculture tree plantations are "green deserts" not forests, say activists. *Mongabay.* Retrieved from http://news.mongabay.com/2008/09/monoculture-tree-plantations-are-green-deserts-not-forests-say-activists/

Hanley, N., Shorgren, J., & White, B. (2013). *Introduction to environmental economics.* Oxford, UK: Oxford University Press.

Howell, S. (2014). "No rights—no REDD": Some implications of a turn towards co-benefits. *Forum for Development Studies, 41*(2), 253–272.

Hudson, R. A., & Hanratty, D. M. (Eds.). (1989). *Bolivia: A country study.* Washington, DC: US Library of Congress.

Humphreys, D. (2006). *Logjam: Deforestation and crisis of global governance.* New York, NY: Routledge.

International Energy Agency. (2010). *World energy outlook 2010.* Paris: Organisation for Economic Co-operation and Development.

Kahn, J., & McDonald, J. (1995). Third-world debt and tropical deforestation. *Ecological Economics, 12,* 107–123.

Kissinger, G., Herold, M., & De Sy, V. (2012). *Drivers of deforestation and forest degradation: A synthesis report for REDD+ policy makers.* Vancouver, Canada: Lexeme Consulting.

Lang, C. (2009, Sept.). Carbon cowboys. *New Internationalist,* p. 29.

Lang, C. (2010, May). Norway-Indonesia forest deal: US$1 billion dollars worth of continued deforestation? *REDD Monitor.* Retrieved from http://www.redd-monitor.org/2010/05/28/norway-indonesia-forest-deal-us1-billion-dollars-worth-of-continued-deforestation/

Laurance, W. (2011, Nov. 17). China's appetite for wood takes a heavy toll on forests. *Yale Environment360.* Retrieved from http://e360.yale.edu/feature/chinas_appetite_for_wood_takes_a_heavy_toll_on_forests/2465/

Lemaitre, S. (2011). Indigenous peoples' land rights and REDD: A case study. *Review of European Community and International Environmental Law* (RECIEL), *20*(2), 150–162.

Lewis, S. L., Edwards, D. P., & Galbraith, D. (2015). Increasing human dominance of tropical forests. *Science, 349*(6250), 827–832.

Lohmann, L. (2009). Regulatory challenges for financial and carbon markets. *Carbon & Climate Law Review, 3*(2), 161–171.

Margarita Declaration. (2014, Aug.). The Margarita Declaration on Climate Change. *REDD Monitor.* Retrieved from http://www.redd-monitor.org/2014/08/08/the-margarita-declaration-on-climate-change-we-reject-the-implementation-of-false-solutions-to-climate-change-such-as-carbon-markets-and-other-forms-of-privatization-and-commodification-of-life/

McAfee, K. (2012). The contradictory logic of global ecosystem services markets. *Development and Change, 43*(1), 105–131.

McDermott, C. L., Coad, L., Helfgott, A., & Schroeder, H. (2012). Operationalizing social safeguards in REDD+: Actors, interests, and ideas. *Environmental Science & Policy, 21*, 63–72.

McMichael, P. (2003). *Development and social change: A global perspective.* Thousand Oaks, CA: Pine Forge.

Morales, J. A., & Sachs, J. (1988). *Bolivia's economic crisis.* Cambridge, MA: National Bureau of Economic Research.

Mustalahti, I., Bolin, A., Boyd, E., & Paavola, J. (2012). Can REDD+ reconcile local priorities and needs with global mitigation benefits? Lessons from Angai Forest, Tanzania. *Ecology and Society, 17*(2), 114–125.

Mutter, R. N., & Overbeek, W. (2011, Oct. 20). *The great lie: Monoculture trees as forests.* United Nations Research Institute for Social Development. Retrieved from http://www.unrisd.org/80256B3C005BE6B5/search/531DAFFB8B319F69 C125792E00499ED1?OpenDocument

Neilson, J., & Leimona, B. (2013). PES and environmental governance in Indonesia. In R. Lyster, C. Mackenzie, & C. McDermott (Eds.), *Law, tropical forests, and carbon,* 207–229. Cambridge, UK: Cambridge University Press.

Ostrom, E. (1992). *Governing the commons: The evolution of institutions for collective action.* Cambridge, UK: Cambridge University Press.

Pandey, C. L. (2014). Climate change agreements: From past to present. *International Journal of Climate Change Strategies and Management, 6*(4), 376–390.

Pandey, C. L. (2015a). Climate change in South Asia: Green bridging between Nepal and India. In I. Watson & C. L. Pandey (Eds.), *Environmental security in the Asia-Pacific,* 95–126. New York, NY: Palgrave.

Pandey, C. L. (2015b). Managing climate change: Shifting roles for NGOs in the climate negotiations. *Environmental Values, 24*(6), 799–824.

Paterson, M., & Grubb, M. (1992). The international politics of climate change. *International Affairs, 68*(2), 293–310.

Peet, R. (2003). *The unholy trinity: The International Monetary Fund, World Bank and World Trade Organization.* London: Zed Books.

Peskett, L. (2013). REDD+ and development. In R. Lyster, C. Mackenzie, & C. McDermott (Eds.), *Law, tropical forests, and carbon,* 230–50. Cambridge, UK: Cambridge University Press.

Rudel, T. K. (2013). The quiet woods: REDD+ in societies with intact rain forests. In R. Lyster, C. Mackenzie, & C. McDermott (Eds.), *Law, tropical forests, and carbon,* 128–50. Cambridge, UK: Cambridge University Press.

Scrieciu, S. S. (2006). Can economic causes of tropical deforestation be identified at a global level? *Ecological Economics, 62*(3/4), 603–612.

Streck, C. (2013). Financial aspects of REDD+: Assessing costs, mobilising and disbursing funds. In R. Lyster, C. Mackenzie, & C. McDermott (Eds.), *Law, tropical forests, and carbon,* 105–127. Cambridge, UK: Cambridge University Press.

Timilsina, G. R., de Gouvello, C., Thioye, M., & Dayo, F. B. (2010). Clean Development Mechanism potential and challenges in Sub Saharan Africa. *Mitigation and Adaptation Strategies for Global Change, 15*(1), 93–111.

United Nations Economic Commission for Europe (UNECE). (2011). *Forest products.* Retrieved from http://www.unece.org/press/pr2011/11tim_p05e.html

United Nations Collaborative Programme on Reducing Emissions from Deforestation and Forest Degradation in Developing Countries (UN-REDD Programme). (2011). *The UN-REDD program strategy 2011–2015*. Retrieved from http://www.unep.org/forests/Portals/142/docs/UN-IMREDD%20Programme%20Strategy.pdf

United Nations Environment Programme. (2007). *Guidebook to financing CDM projects*. Roskilde: CD4CDM. Retrieved from http://www.unep.org/pdf/dtie/FinanceCDMprojectsGuidebook.pdf

United Nations Forum on Forests (UNFF). (2015). *Global objectives on forests*. Retrieved from http://www.un.org/esa/forests/documents/global-objectives/index.html

Wallerstein, I. (1974). *The modern world system: Capitalist agriculture and the origins of the European world economy in the sixteenth century*. New York, NY: Academic Press.

Watson, I., & Pandey, C. L. (2015). *Environmental security in the Asia-Pacific*. New York, NY: Palgrave.

World Bank. (1992). *World development report 1992*. Washington, DC: World Bank.

World Commission on Environment and Development. (1987). *Our common future*. Oxford, UK: Oxford University Press.

World Resource Institute. (1992). *World Resources 1992–93*. Oxford, UK: Oxford University Press.

Wright, T. (2009, July 1). U.S. to forgive Indonesian debt in exchange for conservation plan. *The Wall Street Journal*. Retrieved from http://www.wsj.com/articles/SB124633204676171767

7   Conclusion

Introduction

It is clear that anthropogenic climate change is perhaps the greatest international challenge of the 21st century. In 2012 the World Bank stated that no more than one-third of known reserves of fossil fuels should be consumed before 2050 if the world is to avoid a 2°C increase in the global climate. The World Bank went on to report that unless major technological innovations were widely deployed or a policy change was made, we would not be able to avoid potential climate disasters. Although governments have not made any notable progress in terms of reducing greenhouse gases (GHGs) domestically, the creation of Reducing Emissions from Deforestation and Forest Degradation (REDD) through the United Nations Framework Convention on Climate Change seems to offer a strategy linking climate change and forests. Halting deforestation and forest degradation is important in mitigating emissions of GHGs at a time when climate change negotiations have reached an impasse on other ways of arresting climate change.

The importance of REDD may increase as we understand more fully the unique roles of the forest. Co-benefits of REDD could include carbon sequestration, poverty reduction, and biodiversity conservation, an aspect now recognized by the United Nations Framework Convention on Climate Change and the Convention on Biological Diversity. The core strategy of REDD is to develop a mechanism that aims to halt deforestation through financial incentives. Simply put, if a country agrees to reduce deforestation below a baseline that is agreed with others, it could receive financial compensation. Other countries would financially support this effort because of its contribution to addressing global deforestation trends and climate change in general and, in particular, in return for emissions reduction credits.

There are some basic principles underlying REDD. Countries participate voluntarily in REDD agreements, and payments are made only when performance can be demonstrated through Measurement, Reporting, and

Verification (MRV) processes. It is ascertained that the REDD projects contribute to agreed baselines, and the measured reductions are in terms of halting deforestation or forest degradation, conserving or enhancing carbon stocks, or managing forest sustainably. Developing and least developed countries are in the process of evolving their own national REDD strategies. As an incentive-based mechanism, REDD is defining a new paradigm for forest management in developing countries that is expected to be result oriented and based on performance. Theoretically, REDD is regarded as a smart and cost-effective strategy that could reduce global warming, deforestation, and land degradation in developing countries as well as enhance ecosystem-based adaptation strategies in communities that depend on forest resources. However, despite its promise and potential, few empirical studies have established the efficacy of REDD projects. As we have shown throughout this book, REDD is not the correct approach to addressing climate change. Climate change that results from carbon dioxide being released into the atmosphere, whether from fossil fuel consumption or deforestation, is an important global issue that requires action at the international, regional, national, and local levels.

Forests can play an integral part in mitigating climate change by increasing carbon sequestration and storage capacity. However, one large problem is that we cannot rely too heavily on forests to mitigate climate change as keeping forest intact comes with several repercussions, including greater hardships to the most vulnerable people who live in and around the forest and depend on forest resources for their livelihoods. The two most prominent causes of climate change are the accelerating patterns of energy consumption and the fossil fuel–based capitalistic economic system. Without directly reducing emissions by using integrated approaches to reducing our consumerist patterns and transitioning the gray economic system into a low- or zero-carbon system, any attempt to mitigate climate change is futile, including the mere purchasing of offsets. The current conceptualization of REDD policy ignores the international trade pressures, economic interests, and leakage that lead to deforested landscapes. These pressures come from various factors including agriculture, timber demands, mining, population growth, and economic interests. If forests are expected to play a role in mitigating climate change, they must be used beyond their storage and sequestration capacity. Moreover, the concept of "additionality" that is part of REDD is itself a challenge and controversial. It is really difficult to determine how an existing forest can function to fulfill the role of "additionality," whereas the planting of new forests (monocultures) clearly shows the "additionality." However, this monoculture forest is harmful to the existing biodiversity and ecosystem on the one hand and is driven by short-term unsustainable economic interests on the other. Such forests can stand for about 25 to 50 years. Then they are cut down for sale to make money, releasing a large amount of carbon dioxide into the environment.

As we have shown in the previous chapters, if we fail to utilize forests and their resources appropriately, we encounter the problem of leakage by simply shifting deforestation and forest degradation from one area to other areas, from one country to other countries, from one region to other regions. Ultimately, mitigation of climate change will not occur unless the leakage problem is addressed and sustainable use of forests is achieved. We also need to transition ourselves from a high-consuming society to a low-consuming society and from a carbon-intensive economic system to a low-carbon economy. The question is not only how we can utilize forests to mitigate climate change. Rather, we need to ask ourselves, how can we achieve sustainable forestry? More important, we should ask what kind of policy promotes an ecosystem approach to sustainable forestry and helps to achieve global emissions and poverty reductions. We now turn to providing some potential practices that might help address the problems of forests.

A sustainable forest ecosystem

A sustainable forest ecosystem is a system of vegetation and animals that can naturally support itself without any human interference. Trees are only one feature of the forest ecosystem, albeit the dominant feature. Energy, in the form of light, is captured by leaves in the forest; it is then mixed with carbon dioxide and water before being transformed into plant tissue. The waste of this process is oxygen, which is released into the atmosphere. Forests also purify water by filtering it through soil and litter. The roots of trees are covered with an organism called mycorrhizal fungal filaments, which feed off the roots and in return protect them from disease, promote root-tip growth, and strengthen the ability of roots to take in nutrients from the soil. Without healthy roots, soil turns into infertile dust and sand. A tree's leaves shelter the soil from sun exposure that causes it to dry and from the hammering of raindrops that displaces it. A healthy forest ecosystem can also create its own soil through decay of vegetation. The dead vegetation is broken down by organisms whose only job is decomposition. The creation of soil is the foundation of a sustainable ecosystem because it is the substance through which all vegetation grows. An abundance of vegetation prevents soil erosion and thus allows the soil cycle to stay unbroken. A forest ecosystem is never static because of the ongoing cycle of nutrients and moisture from the air, water sources, and soil. A forest's ability to cope with environmental changes lies in the amount of genetic diversity found within its vegetation and animal species (Berger, 1998, pp. 1–18). The genetic diversity guides each organism's reproduction in order to make changes needed to survive. Outside of these processes are animals that feed off of the vegetation, as well as plant seeds that sprout new vegetation. Some animals protect the vegetation from pests, such as beetles, by feeding off of them.

A healthy forest ecosystem can protect and reproduce itself with minimal human intervention. In addition, it can provide many resources and environmental services for humans. A sustainable forest is much more than the sum of its parts and much more than an ecosystem that captures and stores carbon. Although REDD schemes tout their focus on conserving biodiversity, that is a far second to carbon sequestration and storage. How can a forest be managed to maintain its sustainability and resilience?

Managing a sustainable and resilient forest

Gale and Cordray put forth a definition of sustainability that they refer to as *global village sustainability*. Global village sustainability "reflects a global perspective intent on sustaining the entire earth, both its ecosystems and its human populations" (1991, p. 34). While the authors put forth a definition, they lack a clear method of achieving this type of sustainability. In order to achieve global village sustainability, forests must be seen as having multiple values. They have intrinsic value by just being a forest, and they have utilitarian values such as providing important environmental services like climate stability as well as being a resource for timber and other non-timber products, in addition to supplying biodiverse habitats. Forests should not be reduced to their role in mitigating climate change because it is only one part of their total value.

Among all human activities involved in managing the environment, forestry is particularly unique because of the time scales involved in the production of most tree crops. A short turnover between planting a seed and harvesting can take 50 years for dominant commercial species and more like 60 to 70 years for other species. Forestry is thus a multigenerational task and relies heavily on concrete planning because "resource values, social demands, land-use demands, politics, technology and environmental factors can change drastically with a single crop rotation" (Kimmins, 1992, p. 52). Given the time needed to grow trees, the problem of permanence, or rather lack of permanence, in REDD becomes apparent. Funding must be secured in perpetuity because once the funding is lost, it becomes more profitable to harvest the trees and clear the land for other uses such as growing crops.

According to Cortner and Moote, true ecosystem management occurs when "objectives for land and water resources are related first and foremost to the integrity, vitality, and resilience of ecosystem structures and processes" (1999, p. 1). Ecosystem management must include ecological and socio-economic elements as well as being embedded in a political context. Often the political context and power dynamics of such a situation are not sincerely acknowledged and solved. REDD, as it currently stands, re-creates the power dynamic among developed and developing countries. As we highlighted in chapters 5 and 6, developing countries are secondary and have considerably less power in the context of REDD because they are reliant on the developed countries.

Growing trees and managing an ecosystem are multigenerational public goods that require government regulation of some form. While Cortner and Moote address the issues of involving stakeholders in the decision-making process, they leave the final decision to government bureaucrats in centralized locations away from the forests. The problem is that the people who are most familiar with the forest do not make the final decisions. Also, they do not address the issue of the power the bureaucrats and scientists hold and how that might impact citizens' recommendations. Oliver and Deal argue that "sustainable forestry is too complicated to be achieved through centralized planning and dictating of activities" (2007, p. 154). Centralization leads to inefficiency and an attempt to apply uniform methods to regions that can be diverse (p. 154).

Successful decentralized community-based environmental regulations require several components. First, there needs to be some institutional, government-sanctioned organization that covers the geographical area involved. We will call these forest councils. Next, this organization needs a set of rules and regulations that govern the functioning of the administrative unit. In addition, there needs to be some way to identify stakeholders and ensure their participation in the process. Ensuring participation may require that some stakeholders be subsidized or otherwise supported so that they are able to participate. Finally, there needs to be an equalization of resources, particularly information. Unless all parties are equally prepared to deal with developing forest policy, then any results will be skewed to the benefit of the more powerful (Smith, 2015).

The state would create an outline of regulations that delineate how forest councils are elected and how often they must meet. In such a decentralized system, the state, for political and sovereignty reasons, would have ultimate decision-making authority for approving or disapproving plans for forest management. This would include plans for harvesting of forest resources.

Decentralized community management of forests is the way to encourage the development of the global village model of sustainability. Forests will be managed by the people who have the most intimate knowledge of the forest itself. Locals will be able to implement adaptive management, which allows for "systematic variation by applying specific techniques, monitoring the outcomes, learning from the results, and adjusting the techniques" to better manage the forest (Donoghue & Sturtevant, 2008, p. 14).

Adaptive management is similar to the use of indigenous knowledge, where direct observation of forest health guides forestry practices. The downside to community-based management is that it is inefficient and will require some learning time. There is an inherent learning curve that will continuously exist as techniques are adjusted. There are also costs that will accrue at the federal level because practices will be site-specific, and monitoring will require the same amount of site specificity. Forests will not be able to be judged based on a predetermined definition of ecosystem health. Instead, each ecosystem must be tracked over time to determine its health relative to itself.

The promise and perils of forest certification

In this book we have heavily critiqued using the market to sustain REDD. While market utilization is riddled with problems when it comes to solving environmental problems, markets can be used in a very useful way to protect forests through the certification of sustainable forest management. While it is not a direct link to mitigating climate change, forest certification, through managing forests sustainably, can indirectly assist mitigation efforts. More important, it allows people the continued use of forest resources and does not suffer from leakage problems or lack of financing.

Forest certification provides a method to signal to consumers that a particular good or service meets certain standards. In the case of forest certification, the labels on forest products are meant to signal that the product comes from a forest that is being managed sustainably. Each scheme has specific standards that are used to ensure sustainability; these are usually detailed in their criteria and indicators. The standards of sustainable forest management are created independently. The process of certification is completed by an independent auditor. If the standards are met, the forest receives full certification, and the company or group managing the forest is allowed to use the certification scheme's label. There is also a detailed process for certifying chain of custody, which is meant to follow a forest product from harvest until it reaches an end-product consumer.

The most used and largest certification schemes are the Program for the Endorsement of Forest Certification (PEFC) and the Forest Stewardship Council (FSC). The FSC is backed by non-governmental organizations and smaller groups (often indigenous peoples). The PEFC is mostly supported by large-scale producers. At this time, only a brief overview will be given of the main differences between the two forest certification schemes. The FSC is a non-profit organization registered in Oaxaca, Mexico, and backed by many non-governmental organizations. The PEFC is also a non-profit, but it is a more producer-backed scheme created because the standards of the FSC were thought to be too strict and somewhat unachievable because of the process and unrealistic expectations. The PEFC considers itself to be the largest forest certification scheme. An important difference is that the FSC includes standards for environmental as well as social welfare. Auld, Gulbrandsen, and McDermott (2008) completed a synthesis of much of the forest certification research findings. They found that the FSC was actually able to change the on-the-ground practices of forest managers (p. 198). The PEFC, in contrast, focuses just on the environment and slowly added some social standards much later. It tends to have forests that are certified in countries that do not, on average, have a net forest loss. The FSC, on the other hand, certifies forests in countries with a net forest loss and is working to decrease the rate of deforestation.

Only one of these certification schemes has the potential to create a level playing field among stakeholders. The PEFC leads to a larger imbalance of power because it is dominated by the forestry corporations and producers. The FSC is the preferable method because it attempts to balance the power of multiple stakeholders within its general assembly. The general assembly has three chambers. There is one chamber dedicated to social and indigenous organizations, one for environmental organizations, and another for economic interests. Each member, regardless of the chamber they are in, has one vote. Each chamber holds the same amount of power as the other chambers. Power is balanced even further between the global North and South, or the developed and developing countries. Each chamber is required to have 50 percent of its membership represent the global North and 50 percent represent the global South. Finally, the FSC attempts to remove financial barriers by allowing members of the global South to request financial assistance to attend international meetings (FSC, 2002).

When examining the transparency of the FSC, Auld and Gulbrandsen (2010, p. 98) find that the FSC treats transparency as "an end unto itself," meaning transparency is a key goal of the entity. They examine both procedural and outcome transparency. Procedural transparency involves "openness of governance processes, such as decision-making or adjudication," and outcome transparency involves "openness about regulated or unregulated behaviors," such as the required disclosure of specific information (pp. 99–100).

Clearly, forest certification is not the answer to managing forests to mitigate climate change. We offer it here as a positive step in the right direction. We strongly feel that REDD can be improved and could be made to do what it was intended to do. But that will not happen without major institutional changes. Knowingly or not, the system as it exists allows for many abuses and will not get us where we need to go. We hope that the recommendations discussed herein will help provide movement to improve that system.

Conclusion

To conclude, we note that REDD suffers from two fundamental problems: governance and systemic problems. The governance problem exists in the current REDD policy package that combines offsets with payment for ecosystem services and imposes market-driven neoliberalism on forests, which undermines and monetizes community conservation and social/cultural processes and creates inequalities. This practice tends to force subsistence communities into the cash economy. It prevents much-needed policies that support endogenous, biocultural approaches to biodiversity conservation. It increases land grabs and human rights violations and restricts access to forests, threatening livelihoods and cultural practices. It also causes violence against peasants, indigenous peoples, women, and forest-dwelling communities. Many of these governance issues have been raised by researchers as the fundamental problems affecting the ability of REDD projects to be successful. We concur that these governance problems are important to be addressed for achieving some of the goals of REDD; however, as we demonstrated throughout the book, we believe that systemic issues need serious attention for REDD to be successful. The systemic issues are primarily centered on the consumption patterns of the rich world and the capitalist economic system. Unless our consumption patterns are changed, REDD can achieve very little, as it encourages "leakage" – the movement of deforestation from one place to another – and the neoliberal economic system encourages monoculture tree plantations and genetically modified trees in order to meet cornucopian market demands and economic growth.

Any program like REDD will ultimately fail without fundamental changes in our market economy and dependence on fossil fuels. We do not expect the former to happen, and we suspect that the latter will happen much too late to prevent catastrophic damage to the Earth's atmosphere – at least as far as humans are concerned. As we have said before, REDD is a noble effort and has some limited short-term promise, but it has fundamental flaws that will lead to its failure to seriously reduce carbon in the atmosphere. Nonetheless, we offer here suggestions as to how REDD could be improved and increase the likelihood that it can have an impact – however slight in the long term – on global GHG emissions. First, as we have noted, MRV is expensive. More money and consideration, including oversight, has to be invested in MRV. Given that, currently, MRV is the most expensive part of REDD we are not optimistic that this will happen – but if REDD is to have even limited success, increases in this area are necessary. Second, and this is the most serious problem, the economic incentives to participate in REDD need to be greatly increased. As we have noted, REDD compensation cannot compete with agricultural production – notably palm oil. Unless compensation can compete with market forces for alternative uses of the land in the local economy, then by this measure alone REDD will fail.

Assuming that adequate compensation is paid and appropriate monitoring is performed, the long-term outlook for the planet is not good under a scheme such as REDD as presently constituted. This is because of the permanence problem. Ultimately, stored carbon is released when the trees die or are harvested. The only way a forest conservation program can work is if it is established in perpetuity and if forests are managed so that they remain forests over time. Fortunately, forests know how to do that if we leave them alone. But saving a forest in the short term, only to harvest it 30 or more years later, only forestalls the inevitable and temporarily averts climate disaster. This could be remedied through REDD or some other conservation program if carbon offset funds were used to create land conservation easements or some other mechanism to keep the land as forest or as resilient ecological carbon sinks forever. These measures, although expensive, would serve to protect the rights of indigenous peoples as well as the forest for the long term. Forests could then be managed consistently with the local management systems, such as the forest councils described above.

References

Auld, G., & Gulbrandsen, L. H. (2010). Transparency in nonstate certification: Consequences for accountability and legitimacy. *Global Environmental Politics, 10*(3), 97–119.

Auld, G., Gulbrandsen, L. H., & McDermott, C. L. (2008). Certification schemes and the impacts on forests and forestry. *Annual Review of Environment and Resources, 183*, 187–211.

Berger, J. J. (1998). *Understanding forests*. San Francisco, CA: The Sierra Club.

Cortner, H. J., & Moote, M. A. (1999). *The politics of ecosystem management*. Washington, DC: Island Press.

Donoghue, E. M., & Sturtevant, V. E. (Eds.). (2008). *Forest community connections: Implications for research, management, and governance*. Washington, DC: Resources for the Future.

Forest Stewardship Council (FSC). (2002). *Forest Stewardship Council by-laws*. Retrieved from http://us.fsc.org/download.fsc-international-bylaws.114.pdf

Gale, R. P., & Cordray, S. M. (1991). What should forests sustain? Eight answers. *Journal of Forestry, 89*(5), 31–36.

Kimmins, H. (1992). *Balancing act: Environmental issues in forestry*. Vancouver, Canada: UBC Press.

Oliver, C. D., & R. L. Deal. (2007). A working definition of sustainable forestry. *Journal of Sustainable Forestry, 24*(2), 141–163.

Smith, Z. A. (2015). Collaborative management in natural resources and environmental administration. *Environmental Practice, 17*(2), 156–159.

Index

Printed in the United States
by Baker & Taylor Publisher Services